In Dying We Are Born

The Challenge and the Hope for Congregations

In Dying We Are Born

The Challenge and
the Hope for Congregations

Peter Bush

THE
ALBAN
INSTITUTE
Herndon, Virginia
www.alban.org

The Alban Institute
2121 Cooperative Way, Suite 100
Herndon, VA 20171-5370

Unless otherwise noted, all Scripture quotations are from the New Revised Standard Version of the Bible, copyright © 1989, Division of Christian Education of the National Council of the Churches of Christ in the United States of America, and are used by permission.

Scripture quotations from *The Message*, a paraphrase of the Bible by Eugene H. Peterson, copyright © 1993, 1994, 1995, 1996, 2000, 2001, 2002, are used by permission of NavPress Publishing Group, Colorado Springs, Colorado.

The lines quoted from the poem "Threatened with Resurrection" by Julia Esquivel are from *Threatened with Resurrection: Prayers and Poems from an Exiled Guatemalan*, by Julia Esquivel; copyright © 1982, 1994, Brethren Press, Elgin, Ill., and are reprinted with permission.

The diagrams that appear on pages 24 and 25 are from *To Dream Again: How to Help Your Church Come Alive*, by Robert Dale; copyright © 1981, 2004 Wipf and Stock, Eugene, OR, and are reprinted with permission.

Cover design by Spark Design, LLC.

Library of Congress Cataloging-in-Publication Data

Bush, Peter George, 1962-
  In dying we are born : the challenge and the hope for congregations / Peter Bush.
      p. cm.
  Includes bibliographical references.
  ISBN 978-1-56699-357-9
  1. Church renewal. I. Title.

BV600.3.B875 2007
250—dc22

2007045798

12 11 10 09 08   VG   1 2 3 4 5

Contents

Acknowledgments

For more than seven years I have been thinking about the ideas that are the heart of this book. During that time many people have played a role in deepening my understanding. I wish to acknowledge their influence and support.

My thanks go to the congregation of Knox Presbyterian Church, Mitchell, Ontario, among whose members I was honored to serve for 11 years. In the midst of ministry there I first began to see the power of dying so that God could make alive. Knox also graciously gave me time to read and think, and to write early drafts of parts of this book. Without my time at Knox this book would never have come into being.

The members of the Rural Ministry Study Group, which I was privileged to be part of for more than 10 years, listened patiently to my attempts to put into words the ideas discussed in this book. Their comments and critiques have sharpened my thinking, and the stories they told added to the examples I was gathering. I also presented some of this material at various congregational workshops, and the participants in these groups confirmed the conviction that dying so as to be raised to life is a pattern of God's working in congregations.

Special thanks are due to the Rev. Amanda Birchall, Dr. George Bush, and the Rev. Dr. Christine O'Reilly, who read each chapter of the book, offering their suggestions for improvements and their encouragement to continue the project.

The Alban Institute took the risk of doing this book, and I thank them for that. Beth Ann Gaede is an editor extraordinaire, who with diplomacy noted those places where the point being made was unclear and the argument too theoretical. She was an encouragement when I began to question the value of the project. Thanks to Jean Caffey Lyles, the copy editor, for her skills and wise suggestions for improvements. The entire Alban team has been helpful, going beyond the call in professionalism and patience.

My wife, Debbie Bush, and our son, Nathan, have been supportive and accepting of having an author in the house. Over the last seven years they have been subjected to my endless desire to talk about what I was learning. The phrase "die to live" was heard so often that it has become part of our family vocabulary, having application not only to church life but also in such diverse endeavors as athletics and gardening.

Prologue

Sarah Turner, the minister at St. John's Church, sat in her study replaying last night's meeting in her mind. *What exactly was it that Alec had said? "And I thought we were dead."* He said it immediately after the elders heard how many people had received communion on Easter Sunday. There had been a huge crowd at the Easter service—helium-filled Easter balloons for the children, fifteen young people professing their faith, and the celebration of communion. It had been quite a Sunday—chairs in the aisles and not enough communion cups. Two elders had had to hurry back to the kitchen and fill some cups from the old communion set.

Those were not the things that filled Sarah's mind, however. Rather, she was thinking of Alec's comment. The secretary of the elders' board had reported that 215 people took communion at the Easter service—the largest number to participate in a communion service at St. John's Church in more than fifty years. And then Alec had leaned over to his brother, James, and had stage-whispered, loud enough that half the room could hear, "And I thought we were dead."

It's true, Sarah thought. St. John's had been a tired and apprehensive group of people when she arrived.

St. John's Church was the oldest of the six Christian congregations in Stainton, a community of 3,000 people built on the banks of the Tweedsmuir River in the rich farm country of southern Ontario. Stainton was the business center for the western part of the county, with banks and insurance brokers dominating its main street. On the tree-lined streets north and south of the business core, young families, empty nesters, and retired farmers made their homes. In the surrounding townships, farmers worked the land growing corn, wheat and soya, and white beans, and raised cattle, pigs, and chickens. The local ice arena (home to hockey, ringette, curling, and figure skating), located in the fairgrounds and surrounded by ball diamonds, was a hub of activity for the community.

The history of St. John's went back to the 1840s and the first communion service ever celebrated in Stainton. That service had been held out of doors, with the congregation sitting on makeshift benches. Several members of the present congregation, including Alec and James and their families, had roots in the community and the church that went back to the first service, before there was much of a town, and certainly before a name had been chosen for the church. Over the years, St. John's had experienced its share of ups and downs. The 1980s and early 1990s, however, had felt like a long decline. By the mid-1990s, members had real fears about how much longer the congregation would continue. Sarah understood the depth of this worry only after she had served St. John's for a while.

Sarah had been at St. John's, her second charge, for just over four years. She had served a two-point charge (two yoked congregations) in the Maritime provinces before coming to Stainton, but she enjoyed being able to put all her energy into one congregation rather than feeling that she had divided loyalties. The first years at St. John's had been a blur of activity. Congregational leaders and the congregation itself were open to the suggestions Sarah made, and people willingly poured themselves into new ventures. Using ideas from congregational consultant Charles Olsen's *Transforming Church Boards into Communities of Spiritual Leaders,*[1] a book Sarah read the first summer she was in Stainton, the elders changed their meeting style as they sought to move from following a business model to becoming a spiritual community. The lighting of a Christ candle at the start of elders' gatherings and including corporate prayer and other worship elements in the agenda provided spiritual grounding to the discussions and decision making that were also part of elders' meetings. Elders had changed the way they spoke about the decisions before them, being much more willing to allow spiritual language into the discussion.

Sarah had also challenged the elders to allow laypeople a larger role in leading worship, and elders and others from the congregation had soon begun reading the Scripture lessons. More significant, a worship team was established within a year of Sarah's arrival. This group of four people sat down with Sarah once every six weeks to plan a given worship service. They then led the worship service they had planned, doing everything but the sermon, which they left for Sarah. The worship team went so well that a second team was begun about two years after the first one. The members of the worship teams were developing their gifts and growing in their understanding of worship and of the faith. Every once in a while the question would arise: "Are other churches in the area doing what we are doing? Or are we the only one?" The question never implied that the teams didn't want to do this work anymore; rather, folk were wondering why no other churches were trying this "new thing."

The Sunday school had completely changed, moving to the Children and Worship approach, a Montessori-based church-school program pioneered by Sonja Stewart and Jerome Berryman[2] for younger children, and introducing a new curriculum for the older children. Sarah knew of congregations where such dramatic change in the Christian education program would have led to conflict; St. John's had adapted to the change well, however.

On Tuesdays, a Morning Prayer service was introduced, and a group of eight gathered faithfully. A ministry colleague had said to Sarah, "I don't know any other church in the denomination that does Morning Prayer. How did you persuade the elders to let you do that?"

Then there had been the work with youth. Her first year at St. John's, Sarah had worked with a large confirmation class. She was surprised the following year to find that another group of young people was ready for confirmation. Sarah also put a great deal of energy into a large and difficult-to-control youth group that drew young people from the community. It had been a busy, exciting three years. St. John's had been prepared to take risks and to try new things.

A Surprising Realization

Taking risks to do new things at St. John's meant not only that the congregation was invited to go where it had never been before; it also meant leaving behind things that were well known and comfortable. Congregation members and elders often commented that St. John's was not the way it had been before, that it had changed. The people making the comments were not upset by the changes, but they did know that things were not the way they had been.

As Sarah, who did not use the lectionary to guide her preaching and worship leading, started planning for her third journey from Christmas to Holy Week at St. John's, she decided to do an extended sermon series working through the Gospel of Luke. In her weekly preparations Sarah was caught again and again by a repeated theme. It started with Simeon's words to Mary when the infant Jesus was presented in the temple: "This child is destined for the falling and the rising of many" (Luke 2:34). The theme continued in Jesus's teaching. His discussion of the wide, easy way and the narrow, hard way ended with the words, "[S]ome are last who will be first, and some are first who will be last" (Luke 13:30). Jesus starkly outlined the cost of discipleship a chapter later: "Whoever comes to me and does not hate . . . even life itself, cannot be my disciple" (Luke 14:26). The rejoicing father in the parable of the prodigal son said, "[T]his son of mine was dead and is alive again; he was lost and is found!" (Luke 15:24). Throughout the sermon series Sarah and the congregation of St. John's had been confronted again and again with the theological truth that death leads to life, and that clinging to life would lead inevitably to death. This had certainly been true for Jesus. In Luke his last words on the cross bore witness to his belief that God, his Father, could be trusted to bring life from death: "Father, I place my life in your hands!" (Luke 23:46, *The Message*).

As Sarah worked on the sermon series, she found more evidence of that resurrection hope. She saw it also in the lives of the people of St. John's as she visited them in their homes, met them in the coffee shop, and worked with them at the church. Their faith that death would lead to life was evident in the way they lived their lives with quiet and deep assurance. Alec's words at the elders' meeting, "And I thought we were dead," added a new dimension to the hope of the resurrection for Sarah. *What if the promise of life coming out of death was a promise not just to Jesus, nor just to individual believers, but also a corporate promise? Was it possible for congregations to die and receive new life? Was death leading to life a pattern for communities of faith, not just individuals? And more specifically, was that what had happened at St. John's?* The more Sarah thought about it, the more excited she became about the idea.

Sarah started discussing her idea with ministry colleagues. Some were fascinated by what she was thinking; they told her stories of other congregations that had died and had been given new life. Other colleagues were unhappy with all this talk about congregations dying. It was too negative and depressing to ask congregations to die. The church was to bring hope and joy; this death talk undermined what the church should be saying. Still others wanted to know how a minister could invite a congregation to die so that new life could come and still expect to be paid by a dead congregation. Sarah was not dissuaded by these criticisms. "Die to live" became a phrase that was regularly on her lips. Friends at regional denominational gatherings started to time how long it would take Sarah to make a "die to live" reference in discussions about the issues facing the church. Sarah's son, David, got in on the act, quoting "The last shall be first and the first shall be last" whenever he lost a race with his friends from school.

Sarah's Reflections on her Eighth Anniversary

The eighth anniversary of Sarah's installation as the minister at St. John's gave her the opportunity to take stock. Things were going well; the congregation seemed happy. At St. John's people still seemed open to change. The pulpit had been moved from "eight feet above contradiction" to the same level as the congregation. This change had been well received by the congregation, although three or four people told elders that while they did not oppose the move, they needed time to grieve the loss of what had been. The sanctuary had looked one way for their entire living memory; now it had been changed, and it would take time to get used to the new look. Sarah noted the language of grief and therefore death they had used—and that they also seemed to have a sense of hope looking toward the future.

A slow but steady flow of new people were finding their way through the doors of St. John's. New houses were being built in Stainton as it became a bedroom community for the cities within an hour's drive. Young families with no roots in the community were moving in, drawn by the small-town feel and the recreational opportunities. Some of these new families were making St. John's their church home.

Seeing what was happening at St. John's and in Stainton, Sarah had challenged the elders to do two things. First, she invited them to move the focus of the congregation away from the building. The roof had been replaced, and an elevator had been added. It was time to turn and look out at the community to find ways of reaching the new people who were moving into town. After Sarah first laid out her vision for outreach to the elders, Alec, wise as ever, commented, "What you are asking us to do is more difficult than fixing up the church, isn't it?" With a smile, Sarah agreed that it was. The elders decided to ask a small committee to brainstorm what St. John's could do to reach the new people who were moving to town. When the elders were asked who would volunteer to be on the brainstorming group, a long silence ensued before two elders volunteered with great reticence to be part of the group.

The second challenge Sarah presented to the elders was that they invite some people who had become part of the congregation in the past eight years to join them in leading the church. No one on the elders' board had been in the church for less than fifteen years, and about 30 percent of the Sunday-morning congregation had been part of St. John's for less than eight years. Sarah believed it was essential that a route be opened for some of the new people to step into significant leadership roles in the congregation. A number of the elders, however, had argued that the new people had not yet "done their time," and therefore could not be trusted to lead the church.

The discussions about outreach and leadership had stuck with Sarah. There seemed to have been a change in attitude among the elders. At first Sarah wondered if she was misreading the situation. She was busy with responsibilities that took her out of the congregation on a regular basis. She was spearheading an affordable-housing development in the community, and she had denominational responsibilities at both the regional and national levels. So maybe the problem was that she was not as present for St. John's as she had been eight years earlier. She told herself that when her term on the denomination's ministry committee was finished, she would be able to re-engage, and the sense that things were not quite right would go away.

This self-talk, however, did not silence the quiet voice at the back of her mind saying that something had changed. Sarah decided to pay attention to the voice, taking a day away to think and pray and evaluate. As she spent concentrated time reflecting on St. John's, she identified that recently her suggestions to the elders had not been as well received as they had been earlier in her ministry. Maybe Alec was onto something. She wondered, *Are the changes I am suggesting too difficult?*

When she reflected further, though, she started to realize that the elders were comfortable with the way things were. They saw no reason for the changes she suggested. And it wasn't just congregational leaders who were comfortable with the status quo. In almost every aspect of St. John's life, people seemed willing to settle. The willingness to risk, evident at the beginning of Sarah's ministry, was gone. Sarah wondered: *Does a congregation have to be dead in order to risk? Maybe only congregations that think they are dying are willing to change, knowing they have nothing to lose.*

Ministry had been more fun, more exhilarating, when people were not comfortable with the way things were, when leaders knew that things had to change. Sarah had been reading C. S. Lewis's Narnia series to her son, David, and a line from *The Last Battle* rang in her head: "Come farther up, come farther in!"[3] Sarah wanted that to be the motto of her ministry, and right now St. John's did not seem interested in going any farther. Sarah returned from her day away convinced that she had identified the problem, but unsure how to address the challenge, unsure how to tell the elders what she was thinking and feeling.

Four months after her day away, a series of events confirmed Sarah's analysis of retrenchment at St. John's. Philip, a widower in the congregation whom Sarah had befriended, died. In his will Philip left the residual of his estate, after bequests to relatives, to St. John's. The finance people at St. John's were pleased that Philip had thought of the church, but they did not have great expectations. Philip and his wife, who were childless, had lived a hard life on a farm west of Stainton. When they retired from the farm, they bought a modest home in town. About two months after receiving the news that the church was a beneficiary of Philip's estate, Sarah got a call from the lawyer's office to come and pick up an envelope. Sarah went and signed for the envelope. Upon opening it, she found a check for $389,000, the residual of Philip's estate. Sarah walked back to the church in a daze. She called the chair of the congregational trustees to tell her the good news. From there the news of Philip's generosity spread like wildfire. Suddenly everyone at St. John's was in shock.

Everyone also had an idea about what to do with the money— build an addition to the church, complete with a "ladies' parlor"; sock the money away for a rainy day; fix all the stained-glass windows in the church building—and the list went on and on. Sarah, together with two influential elders, persuaded the rest of the elders that the congregation should tithe on the estate. A small committee was established to determine how best to give away $38,900, one-tenth of the money. The committee settled on a development project in rural Thailand. The elders took the recommendation to the congregation, which voted overwhelmingly in favor of the project. Then members of the finance committee started raising concerns about the decision-making process: they had not been sufficiently consulted; the congregation did not have the right to make this decision. And what if St. John's needed the money in the future? Finally, two months after receiving clear instructions from the congregation, the treasurer sent the check.

Over the next year Philip's estate became the unnamed elephant in the room at virtually every elders' meeting, and certainly in any discussion of vision, the future, and long-range planning. If it had been difficult before to get the elders to think about new initiatives, it was virtually impossible now. They had no interest in taking risks. At the congregational level people were less and less willing to throw themselves into programs and activities. In conversations Sarah had with key leaders in the congregation she sensed an undercurrent of frustration and at times even anger. Sarah also felt that she herself was drifting. Her ministry seemed directionless. She felt that she was just going through the motions. *What on earth is going on?* Sarah wondered.

She started rethinking her "die to live" idea. If this was what happened when dead congregations came back to life, she wasn't at all sure that dying to live was a good thing. What if St. John's *hadn't* died? Maybe the congregation had just been close to death. If the congregation hadn't died, then what was going on in the congregation wasn't really new life. Sarah took some comfort in that thought. She could not imagine that resurrection should make people so unhappy. *If what is happening at St. John's is what happens in congregations that think they are alive, then I would sooner do ministry in a dying congregation,* Sarah said to herself more than once.

Sarah spent hours thinking about, fretting about, praying over what was happening. One day while driving home from a hospital visit in the nearby city, she recalled the elders' meeting the month after the check from Philip's estate had arrived. Kathrine had said, "Philip was so appreciative of all that we at St. John's did, especially the way we cared for his wife when she was dying." It came to Sarah in a flash:

The people of St. John's think they earned that money; they don't see it as surprising grace. They think they have pulled themselves up by their own bootstraps. They think they have created the new life.

Sarah mused, Being a leader at St. John's was now a good thing. The congregation was a comfortable place to be, and now it had financial resources. There was prestige involved in being part of the congregation, with leading the congregation, with making decisions in the congregation. *St. John's thinks it is alive.* Sarah saw that since the leaders believed they were at least partially responsible for the new life, they also believed that they had the right to control that life, and the elders had taken it upon themselves to ensure that the congregation would be protected from anything that might challenge its newfound life. They had moved from being willing to risk, because they had nothing to lose, to clinging to what they had because they now had something to lose. How, Sarah wondered, was she going to help the elders at St. John's understand that they still had nothing to lose, *because the life the congregation does have is not ours? How do we, as leaders and as a congregation, learn to die every day?*

As Sarah mulled all of these thoughts over for the next while, uncomfortable questions began to emerge: Maybe it wasn't just the elders who needed to die to their plans and dreams, to their desire to be in control, to their sense of who St. John's was. *What if I have to die to my plans, my agenda, my desire to be right? Have I done the same thing the elders have done? Have I started to assume that St. John's is alive because of my hard work? Have I started to accept credit for what is happening at St. John's?* But having *identified* the spiritual question that needed to be asked did not mean that she knew how to *answer* the question. How could she remain dead and still be a leader of a congregation? How could she hold loosely to her ministry at St. John's and still be fully engaged in doing that ministry?

Sarah was more convinced than ever that "die to live" was the spiritual path congregations needed to take. She also knew from hard experience that "die to live" was not only for congregations that thought the end was near. "Die to live" was a pattern of life that the leaders of all congregations, even those that thought they were alive and well, needed to adopt. Sarah felt energized by this discovery. Learning to die and teaching the elders to die would not be easy, but the aimlessness she had been experiencing in her ministry was gone. She had a new sense of purpose in her work.

CHAPTER 1

A Review and Critique of Some Models of Congregational Renewal

Many observers of the church in North America contend that the church is in decline. They point to congregations with fewer people in the pews on Sunday than there used to be, and they note that in many churches those who attend are grayer than the general population. Beyond the numbers, the cause of much hand-wringing, a malaise verging on despair grips the hearts of many congregational and denominational leaders. The litany of woe about the North American church has been recounted so often that the only new material added with each telling is the data cited in support of the author's or speaker's case. It would be wearisome to travel this well-marked road yet one more time.

This doomsaying regarding the church, however, comes from a perspective centered in the West. A larger view of the world reveals that the church in Africa, in Central and South America, and in much of Asia is doing well and seeing remarkable growth in many places. While this broader view does not reduce the anxiety about the future of a given congregation in a Western society, it does challenge the flat statement "The church is in decline."

Most of the authors who document the decline of the Western church go beyond simply describing the contours of that decline; they also attempt to diagnose the problem. Among the causes cited:

- materialism and hyper-consumerism,
- the privatization of religious expression,

- greater competition for people's time,
- a wider range of paths through which to express one's spirituality,
- loss of confidence in the church's faith,
- inability to move beyond the narrow confines of a naive faith,
- overcommitment to the traditions of the church,
- lack of commitment to the traditions of the church,
- biblical illiteracy and a lack of expositional preaching,
- disconnection from postmodern culture and the missional opportunities it provides, and
- fear that any change from the status quo will only make things worse.

Readers will notice the contradictory nature of some of the diagnoses. Having diagnosed the problem, most authors go on to propose a cure. Observing the many books being published on the subject, Michael Jinkins, associate professor of pastoral theology at Austin Presbyterian Theological Seminary, Austin, Texas, comments, "The literature on the church's decline seems to be the only thing growing in North American Protestantism. And it is a literature riding the crest of a tidal wave of anxiety that threatens everything in its path."[1] Of proposed solutions there seems to be no end. It quickly becomes wearisome to keep track of each new panacea.

Perhaps by proposing solutions, the commentators are demonstrating an additional factor in the church's decline. Deeply ingrained in Western culture is the belief that every problem has a solution. The church is no different from the culture in this belief. Somewhere there is a plan that, if initiated, or a technique that, if used, would stop the decline and return the church to its former status. Maybe no program or technique will turn the tide. Readers will know of congregations whose leaders went to every workshop trumpeting yet another system that would lead to congregational turnaround. The congregation implemented program after program and technique after technique, but the decline did not end. In the end the congregation's epitaph reads, "The solutions attempted were a complete success, but unfortunately the patient died."

A well-known version of the Prayer of St. Francis of Assisi contains the line, "And in dying we are born to eternal life." A number of authors have begun to suggest that the church in North America needs to die so that it can be reborn. This bold suggestion takes seriously the centrality of the resurrection for the Christian faith. As Michael Jinkins writes in his book *The Church Faces Death*: "When the church faces death, in point of fact, it encounters a critical moment when it may know the power of resurrection. But the church can only know this power in actually facing its death."[2] The church must understand that its death is possible—is, in fact, inevitable. Only then can the church experience the amazing power of the resurrection. In his important book *Soul Tsunami: Sink or Swim in New Millennium Culture*,[3] Leonard Sweet, professor of postmodern Christianity and popular speaker, argues that the postmodern world is full of "double rings"—two seemingly contradictory ideas held in balance with one another. The balance is maintained not by trying to create some compromise between the opposites, but rather by affirming that the two concepts are contradictory and yet both true. Examples of double rings in popular culture are "the global village" and "simple abundance." A number of double rings are to be heard in the teachings of Jesus, such as "The last shall be first and the first shall be last" and "If you want to find your life, lose it." In conversation with Sweet, I suggested that the subtitle to *Soul Tsunami* should have been "Sink to Swim." Sweet agreed. The paradox of being able to swim only after drowning fits the "double ring" theme of the book.

For the church facing its death, confronting the reality of death by drowning should not be a cause for fear. G. K. Chesterton, an apologist for Christianity in the first third of the twentieth century and the creator of the Father Brown mysteries, neatly summed up the hope by which the church lives. Christianity, Chesterton wrote, "had a god who knew the way of the grave."[4] With faith in a God like that, being put in the grave should not cause fear among Christians. Chesterton argued that at least five times the church appeared to be dead, but each time it was brought back to life. The Yale church historian Kenneth Latourette wrote that the ebb and flow of the church's advance are like the rising tide of the ocean.[5] A wave advances and then retreats, seeming to lose ground, but the crest of the next wave reaches further up the beach, before it too retreats, to be superseded by another wave, and so on. What takes place in just seconds with ocean waves may take dozens, even hundreds of years with the church. A long period of advance may give way to a long decline, including the death of congregations and even the seeming death of the church as a whole. But, Latourette argued, if we take the long view, we see that the history of the church is one of advance. Andrew Walls, widely respected missiologist and church historian, adds credence to Latourette's view when he speaks of the cyclical nature of the church's history, a series of deaths and resurrections.[6] Even though this pattern can be seen at the macro-level of church history, however, few congregational renewal advocates suggest that a congregation's death is the way for it to find new life.

Models of Congregational Renewal

Most North American congregations take neither the broad, global view nor the long, historical view of the church's rise and fall and subsequent rise. Consequently, they live with a high level of anxiety, which they attempt to address by trying various renewal strategies. In determining which renewal strategy to use, local congregational leaders rarely evaluate a proposal on the basis of the author's underlying assumptions or theological understanding of church. Instead the questions asked concern how different the renewed congregation will look from the present congregation, and the cost—financial, spiritual, psychological—of that change. The myriad solutions suggested by church-revitalization experts fall into one of two broad categories. The first group of experts believes that the church has only a mild illness and that, with proper attention, the local congregation can become healthy again. The subtitle to a book by Aubrey Malphurs, professor at Dallas Theological Seminary, illustrates why local church leaders like proposals in this first category: "How to Change a Church without Destroying It."[7] A second group of thinkers, however, believe that many congregations are seriously ill and can be transformed only by radical change. Congregational leaders need to be desperate before they are willing to explore changing the congregational culture.

BUILDING ON WHAT YOU'VE GOT

Congregational renewal advocates who contend that most congregations are not at death's door propose that congregations should "build on what you've got." In the process of building on what is already present, the congregation will be transformed.

Kennon Callahan's *Twelve Keys to an Effective Church* outlines the elements churches need to possess to become effective in the broadest definition of "effective." Six relational characteristics assist the church in its "mission with persons who have specific human hurts and hopes."[8]

1. Specific, Concrete Missional Objectives
2. Pastoral and Lay Visitation
3. Corporate, Dynamic Worship
4. Significant Relational Groups
5. Strong Leadership Resources
6. Streamlined Structure and Solid, Participatory Decision Making

Also listed are also six functional characteristics of effective churches:

7. Several Competent Programs and Activities
8. Open Accessibility
9. High Visibility
10. Adequate Parking, Land, and Landscaping

11. Adequate Space and Facilities
12. Solid Financial Resources

Callahan has done further work on these keys, determining that small churches need not work on all twelve, but rather can choose eight of the twelve strengths to do well. A quick review of the twelve keys indicates how North American this list is. For example, parking is not a concern for 90 percent of the world's Christians as they consider attending worship. They have no cars to park. That aside, one of the strengths of Callahan's approach is that it moves congregations from thinking about what they are not good at (things that cause congregational dissatisfaction) to focusing on what congregations do well (things resulting in congregational satisfaction), and doing those even better. This approach enhances congregational self-esteem, a central concern in much contemporary writing about congregational life. The key to becoming an effective congregation, Callahan argues, is for the leadership to identify two things the church is good at and to do them even better. Then leaders are to select two characteristics the congregation is struggling with, but which would be "fun" to improve, and add them to the list of things on which to focus. Congregations are to proceed in this fashion until they have developed all twelve characteristics (eight for small congregations). "Fun" is important for Callahan. Being part of the leadership of the church should be fun; taking on new initiatives should be fun.

Callahan brings more than forty years of consultancy work, along with hands-on pastoral experience, to his discussion. Recognizing that the church is different from the business community, he calls on church leaders to trust God rather than relying on demographic projections and marketing strategies. He writes, "This reliance on God is prayerful and powerful. It is strange to me that so many long-range planning committees do not pray. . . . They discuss their options for the future more like amateur sociologists than 'called-of-God Christians.' And they wonder why they fail."[9] Callahan is critical of the excessive doomsaying of the North American church, asserting, "In coming years, we need more churches that are interested in success and fewer churches that are preoccupied with their own problems."[10] He argues that too many congregations in North America are "locked in a closed tomb," unable or unwilling to see that they have been made alive by the risen Christ.

Callahan's insights are helpful. Many congregations have failed to understand that they have nothing to fear, because in the resurrection of Jesus Christ all fear is gone. But are congregations that are completely focused on themselves "locked in a closed tomb"? Many congregations have not yet been in the tomb. They do not understand that they are dead. Clinging to the last bits of what they have come to know as the life of the church, they are unwilling to hold a funeral. Many congregations do not realize that in their baptism they have died and have been raised to life again. Through their actions congregational leaders deny that they are dripping wet from the waters of baptism.

A dead congregation learns to pray with Jesus, "Not my will, but thine be done." Congregations that know they are going to die will move from seeking their own survival to seeking God's reign. Aware that they are wet from the waters of baptism, they are unconcerned about their future. Understanding that they have nothing to lose, these congregations see risking all for God as no great threat. Leaders of "dead congregations walking" do not spend time devising plans to cut costs or to make more efficient use of their resources; rather, they spend time waiting on God (in prayer, in silence, in expectation of what God will do). They have no empire to build, no legacy to leave; the future is entirely in God's hands. While a given congregation may cease to exist, Jesus' promise remains: even the gates of hell will not prevail against the church universal. Dead congregations have had a change in their outlook; no longer is it *all about them*; rather it is all about the expansion of the reign of God and the advance of Christ's church.

Afraid of dying, many congregations do everything in their power to avoid death, seeking to maintain the little bit of life they have, struggling to survive. Yet the only way out of the tomb is to die; only then can God raise the congregation. Thus Callahan's twelve keys make sense in congregations that know their life is not their own. The twelve keys help churches that have already died to become effective. Congregations that have not yet died and grasp the twelve keys as a way to maintain congregational life, however, run the risk of missing out on the new life that awaits congregations that are dead and prepared to admit they are dead.

A second group of proponents of "build on what you've got" are Christian Schwarz and the Natural Church Development movement.[11] Schwarz examined a thousand congregations around the world to discover the keys that lead to healthy, growing congregations. He discovered eight characteristics, set forth in his book *Natural Church Development*:

1. Empowering Leadership
2. Gift-oriented Ministry
3. Passionate Spirituality
4. Functional Structures
5. Inspiring Worship Service
6. Holistic Small Groups
7. Need-oriented Evangelism
8. Loving Relationships

Schwarz argues that all eight characteristics must be present for a church to be healthy. By the use of a set of surveys, a congregation's strength in each area can be determined and graded. Schwarz insists that any church scoring 65 percent or higher on each of the eight factors will grow. In distinction from Callahan, Schwartz argues that churches must find their weakest characteristic and work at raising that "minimum factor."

Natural Church Development proponents contend that congregations are living organisms. The word "biotic" is a central piece of the vocabulary. Living organisms have interdependent parts; their cells multiply; there is a symbiosis among the parts. Most important, for

Schwarz, all living organisms grow. He asserts that this understanding will transform how most congregational and denominational leaders think about church. A truth about living organisms that Schwarz does not discuss is that living things age, decline, and die. If the "biotic" principle is central to understanding the healthy church, then Natural Church Development advocates need to find a way to talk about the decline and death of congregations. Death is part of nature and therefore must be part of all natural development, including church development. The life and growth of the church are not something the church creates. The church is given life not by nature but by God. The life of the church in Acts was not natural; it was supernatural. Hope had died. The despair of the disciples was transformed not by a natural process but by a supernatural one. Natural Church Development leaves little room for *Supernatural* Church Development. Natural growth cannot make the dead alive.

Presentations on Natural Church Development often leave congregations believing that the characteristics are a guaranteed prescription for success. I have talked with congregational leaders who, having attended Natural Church Development workshops, observed that the approach was introduced as if it were a magic talisman that would work every time, in every situation, producing spectacular growth. Such a presentation seems to overlook an important fact, however: God is free to be God, independent of any human action or planning. The reality remains that the church is not ours; it is God's. God fundamentally wants the body of Christ to grow and expand to reach all people with the amazing news about Jesus Christ. Sometimes the God-given growth, as with the grain of wheat that must fall into the ground and perish before it sprouts, must be preceded by death. Only then can God make it alive.

A third "build on what you've got" model of congregational renewal is the best-practices approach taken by the authors of *Discovering Hope: Building Vitality in Rural Congregations*.[12] Shannon Jung, a Presbyterian with a passion for rural congregations, and David Poling-Goldenne, who at the time the book was published was director of congregational ministries for the Evangelical Lutheran Church in America, drew together teams of people from 26 effective rural and small-town congregations and asked what they were doing right. They identified six "best practice" areas:

- Prayer
- Worship
- Disciple-making
- Evangelism
- Caring Ministries
- Leadership

These six best practices are lived out by a local congregation within a particular context and will therefore take on different shapes, depending on location. The purpose of the best practices is to advance the mission of Jesus Christ in the local community and beyond. Two challenges face congregations seeking to build on the learning gathered together in *Discovering Hope*. First, this is not a quick fix. Changing and enhancing the practices of a congregation will transform the congregation over the long haul. But congregational leaders often turn to *Discovering Hope* when they are desperate for a solution to their church's decline. They are disappointed to find that it is not a program designed to "save" the church. Jung and Poling-Goldenne understand that the transformation of congregations is a long-term process built on prayer and dedicated leadership. Not without reason, the first "best practice" discussed is prayer, and the last is leadership. The second challenge is that changes in practice require the death of one way of doing things and the raising up of a new way of living out the faith. While changes in practice may not produce rapid change in the life of the congregation, over time they can transform a church. Congregational leaders may look at the six practice areas saying to themselves, "We are already doing things in those areas, so this will not mean much change in our church's life. We can control this change." As the Spirit of God begins to act through the changes in practice, some leaders may indicate that they did not agree to the cultural shifts. Resistance to changes in the congregation's identity highlights how rooted congregations can become in a particular self-understanding.

Discovering Hope and the other "build on what you've got" models do not sufficiently account for the difficulty of changing a congregation's culture. Jesus said, "No one sews a piece of unshrunk cloth on an old cloak; otherwise, the patch pulls away from it, the new from the old, and a worse tear is made" (Mark 2:21). Changing the culture of a congregation so that it is open to the transforming life of the Spirit takes more than a few patches; it requires a radical new life, a life that can be found only by dying so that God can bring new life.

TEAR DOWN AND START AGAIN

A second group of congregational renewal advocates contends that things are seriously wrong in the North American church and that many congregations need heart transplants. Heart transplants involve killing the patient (stopping the heart) to give the patient new life. This second group of renewal advocates is not convinced that anything can be salvaged from existing congregations upon which to build. The group contends that the church should "tear down the existing congregational culture and start again."

Some in this group of writers use the human life cycle as a metaphor to explain what they believe needs to happen in congregations. In his important book *To Dream Again: How to Help Your Church Come Alive,* the pastoral theologian Robert Dale outlines the congregational life cycle.[13] From its birth with a *dream,* through the articulation of congregational *beliefs* and the development of *goals* and a *structure* and on to actual *ministry,* the congregation is on the upward side of the life cycle. Just as an individual cannot stay at peak physical condition, so the organization, the church, begins to decline, through *nostalgia, questioning, polarization,* and finally to *dropout* (death). All of these are on the downward side of the life cycle. Dale argues that

a congregation cannot climb back up the curve once it has reached *nostalgia* or *questioning* or has gone even further toward death. The only way out of decline is to begin a new "dreaming cycle," moving to the upside of the curve and riding that *dream* through *beliefs*, *goals*, and *structure*, and on to *ministry*. Once things start to slip into decline, it is time to begin again with another dream. Dale describes three ways congregations can respond to being on the downside of the life cycle.

Some leaders, immobilized by the decline and believing they are unable to do anything to stem the decline, choose to do nothing. Other leaders, knowing the ship is in trouble, are willing do anything and everything to stop it from sinking. Often "doing anything" leads to a shotgun approach to church life; instead of being focused, the impact is diffuse and unclear. A third response, the one Dale advocates, is for leaders to do something. They must "dream again." Focusing their energy on this one goal will give the leadership the ability to begin again.

Alice Mann, an Alban Institute consultant, in her provocatively titled book *Can Our Church Live? Redeveloping Congregations in Decline,* uses a model similar to Dale's.[14] After the *birth* and *formation* of the congregation comes a period of *stability.* Eventually a point is reached at which *decline* begins. If that *decline* is sensed early enough, congregational leaders can, through ongoing renewal, move the congregation to a point fairly high on the upside of the cycle.

If the *decline* has become well entrenched, Mann argues, then much more serious action, *revitalization* of the congregation, must be sought, which will land it further down the left-hand side of the curve, closer to a new birth. Finally, if the congregation is near death,

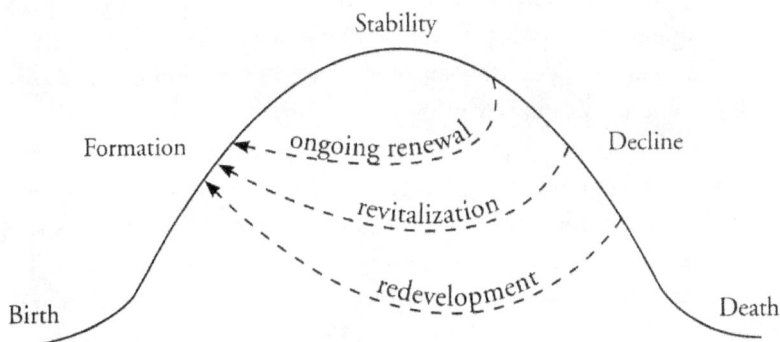

then *redevelopment* is the only answer, as virtually everything within the congregation is formed anew.

Both Dale and Mann are uncompromising: many congregations in North America are in trouble and may be near death. Mann writes, "If a congregation never replaces the blame response with a learning stance, or if it waits too long to try something new, death is the likely result. But death does not come easily. Denial and blame . . . become the enemies of a holy death."[15] Trying something new, for Dale and Mann, is not merely a matter of tinkering with what is already present; rather, congregations need to be renewed, revitalized, or redeveloped, all of which require significant transformation of the congregation's life and systems. Believing that congregations can dream again, and can reach those dreams, these authors are hopeful.

Mann and Dale speak of the death of a congregation as the end of the life-cycle curve. Death is inevitable unless a congregation is renewed, revitalized, or redeveloped. I believe that moving to the upside of the life cycle (dreaming again, renewal, revitalization, redevelopment—whatever words are used to describe this transition) also requires a death. To begin again means dying to what has been. The old dream, no matter how worn out and broken it appears, is still a dream that led to effective ministry at one time. Moving to the other side requires burying that dream, so that a new dream can be born. This movement is a death. Any death, including a death that ends a congregational dream, is painful.

Death in a congregation may be experienced both personally and corporately. For example, congregational leaders who start down the path of revitalization may discover that in the revitalized congregation they no longer have a leadership role. Their passions and gifts may not fit the new dream. Congregations that dream again may find that the new dream given by God calls on them to remove the organ and pulpit. This remodeling of the sanctuary is a death, as one way of being the church is replaced by another. The English-speaking congregation that built the church building and therefore feels ownership of the building may find itself displaced from the sanctuary by the rapidly growing Mandarin-speaking congregation.

Meeting in the church hall instead of the sanctuary requires a death
for the English-speaking congregation. In each of these cases, a new
dream, redevelopment of some kind, has taken place, but a death
preceded the new life. As a congregation goes past Ministry (Dale)
or Stability (Mann), death—either the death that lies at the end of
the life cycle or the death that precedes the coming of new life—is
the inevitable result.

Brian McLaren, pastor and widely published author, describes the
congregational redevelopment that led to the formation in 1987 of
Cedar Ridge Community Church, located between Washington, D.C.,
and Baltimore. McLaren went to the congregational leadership:

> I suggested we make an abrupt, discontinuous change. . . . "I propose
> that we go to the church and tell them we would like to disband. . . .
> We'd spend the next ten months in a gestation period, an incubation
> period, going back to ground zero to come up with a new mission
> statement and a strategy. . . . We'd train our people to become the core
> of a whole new kind of church. . . ." We led our church through a ten-
> month gestation period. We moved to a new location, took on a new
> name, and developed a whole new philosophy of ministry.[16]

This story is about the death and raising up of a congregation.
McLaren, however, never uses that language; rather, the congregation
"disbands" and is reinvented. The reinvented church is not in continuity with the previously existing congregation, having a new name, a
new location, and a new philosophy of ministry (a new dream). This
is a resurrected congregation. Why then not use the metaphor of death
and resurrection? Is such language too frightening? Does speaking of
"redevelopment" and "reinvention" give leaders a sense that they are
in control? Death is frightening. Congregations do not want to die,
do not want to be told that the only way to live is to die, and do not
want to acknowledge that they, too, will one day die.

If congregations are death-averse, congregational leaders are even
more so. In North American culture, leaders are people with a plan.
Dale argues that congregational leaders need to initiate a new planning

cycle, which will lead to a new dream, moving the congregation from the downside of the life cycle to the upside. By focusing on finding a new plan to initiate, however, leaders may fail to experience deeply the pain of the congregation's death. Congregational leaders are called to die with the congregation, so that God can make them, together with the congregation, alive. When congregational leaders are prepared to "come and mourn awhile" with the congregation, they have the credibility to speak of hope.

Congregational leaders whose ears are open will hear a double ring as they mourn the death of the congregation. On the one hand, they are people of faith who know that God can and will raise the dead to life again. Such faith, however, may lead to demands that God act in ways that fit human plans, rather than to recognition of God's freedom of action. On the other hand, leaders know that there is nothing they can do to cause the congregation to be raised to life again. Such an honest assessment of human impotence may lead to passivity and despair, however. In exploring congregational and denominational revitalization, leaders need to ensure that they are hearing both notes of the double ring: seeking the renewal of the congregation and waiting on God to act. Although McLaren went to his congregation's leaders with a plan, his tentative language and uncertainty in describing the new church signaled his awareness that the only One who can bring the congregation to life again is the One who called the congregation into being in the first place.

In their book *Redeveloping the Congregation,* Mary Sellon, Daniel Smith, and Gail Grossman, who did redevelopment work together and independently for ten years before writing their book, recognize the death-and-resurrection aspect of congregational redevelopment:

> Redevelopment is what the journey is called when the congregation has fundamentally congealed. . . . The congregation's God-given energy flows almost totally towards its own survival. When the faith community walls itself off from its community rather than living to serve it, death is inevitable. The only question is whether there will be

life for that congregation on the other side of death. . . . Redevelopment is the resurrection journey. Like a bone marrow transplant or
stem cell replacement, much of what seems intrinsic to the church
will have to die.[17]

The authors recognize that death is "inevitable" and that redevelopment is not pain-free. A bone-marrow transplant is painful for both
donor and recipient. The road to resurrection is not easy. The authors'
courage in using such tough language is to be applauded. My concern
centers on this question: How much space does this description leave
for the surprising, uncontrollable, completely free action of the Spirit
of God? The concern is not whether Sellon, Smith, and Grossman
recognize the importance of the surprising grace of the Spirit, which
they do, but whether their readers will understand that all human
effort to redevelop a congregation is just so much dust in the wind
without the gracious action of God. Raising the dead is beyond the
ability of human beings. All we can do, in our limited human fashion,
is to prepare congregations for new life by nurturing an expectation
of resurrection and modeling trust in the all-wise and all-loving God
who will do what is best.

Stephen Compton, a new-church development consultant,
recognizes the inability of human leaders to bring new life to dead
congregations. He argues that congregational leaders should not even
try to turn "congealed," inward-looking congregations around. The
best thing to do is to let these congregations die.[18] For Compton the
future hope of the church resides in the planting of new congregations.
Therefore the resources, financial and human, used to maintain dying
congregations should instead be put into starting new communities of
faith. Compton uses the congregational life cycle to argue that death is
as natural a part of life as birth, and that denominational leaders need
to have the courage to take congregations off life support. Compton
is right that planting new congregations is one of the most important
activities for the church in North America to do. He is also correct in
noting that the resources to do that work are often squandered in the

support of congregations that are kept alive for reasons that have little
to do with God's hopes for humanity. The tough love of turning off
the financial tap and confronting these congregations with the hard
reality that they are dying does not signal that there is no hope for
these churches. It would be possible to hear in Compton no room for
hope for dying congregations. Yet hope survives, the hope of resurrection; for the death of one congregation may lead to new seeds being
planted and new congregations being started. This is one of the ways
whereby God may raise a dead congregation to life.

Church-renewal consultants Bill Easum and Tom Bandy are to
be found at a barbecue serving up gourmet burgers made from sacred cows as the band warms up in the background for the dinosaur
dance to follow.[19] Easum and Bandy—partners in Easum, Bandy,
and Associates[20]—have become an influential team calling for a
radical reorientation of the church. Easum raises the challenge: "Is
the congregation willing to focus ministry primarily on passing on
the new life in Christ, or is the church focused primarily on its own
survival?"[21] Given the end of both Christendom and modernity, the
way ahead is for the church to turn from its inward-looking survivor
mentality to an outward-focused, life-risking ministry in a broken and
hurting world. This fundamental reorientation will require leaders to
give up control of the ministry of the church (the focus of Easum's
Sacred Cows Make Gourmet Burgers) and to break ministry-destroying
habits (the focus of Bandy's *Kicking Habits*).[22] Bandy and Easum state
bluntly that the North American church has lost its passion for mission. Congregational leaders often miss the point that the recovery of
the church's mission is central to what Bandy and Easum are saying;
instead they become preoccupied with the structural changes the two
authors advocate. In their most recent work, both Bandy and Easum
are less categorical in their structural prescriptions for addressing the
church's "sickness unto death," recognizing that there are "no rules,
only clues" for life in the "Christian chaos" that is church life "on the
other side" of the wormhole.[23] The focus of their writing continues to

be transforming the church from an institution into a community of faith, reorienting its purpose from self-preservation to the transformation of people's lives.

Easum and Bandy are too quick, however, to move to solutions for the church. The addict, to use Bandy's metaphor, must hit rock bottom before being willing to find a new way. For a shocking number of addicts, rock bottom means death: the death of their employment, their family relationships, their status in the community, and even at times their physical death. Notably Bandy never writes of death's being part of the process by which habits are kicked. He does not acknowledge that for transformation to take place, the old must die.

The death of the old is a process that cannot be hurried if the new resurrection life is going to be appreciated for the miracle of grace it is. Although there is danger in leaders' lingering too long at the congregational deathbed, it is important that time be taken to feel the pain of death and to understand that new life cannot be created by mere human beings. When people are changed, "everything old has passed away; see, everything has become new!" (2 Cor. 5:17). The old dies, and a new reality is born.

Although both Bandy and Easum are clear that the church's mission is to pass on the new transforming life of Christ, they suggest a planning process to transform the church's orientation that requires the church to listen more closely to the culture than it does to the Spirit of God. In fairness to Easum and Bandy, they correctly argue that the call of God is heard through the brokenness of the culture and of individuals in the culture. But the consumer is not always right. Although those within the congregation who control the congregational system must be removed from power, replacing them and giving control to a new group of people—this time the potential consumers—is not a marked improvement. The church is called, at times, to stand against the cultural norms in ways that will make it unpopular. Sometimes the church must be countercultural. That is one way it is called to risk its life.

There Is More than One Way to Die

Congregations in rural areas, towns, urban cores, and suburbs are dying. In many of these congregations people are preparing for the funeral. Other congregations in these same communities appear to be doing fine, continuing to pay the bills; weekly worship is taking place. Yet even in these congregations, all is not well. For new life, new energy, new passion to arise, these congregations must also die—die to one way of being the church so that a new way of being the church can arise.

Two types of congregational death are possible. Some congregations need to close their doors, bringing an end to years of ministry. Such a death means that the congregation is no more. Other congregations need to dramatically change their culture and ways of doing ministry. Such a drastic change may not entail the literal closing of the doors, but it will require people to give up deeply held understandings of the life and purpose of the congregation. This, too, is a death.

Only by dying will a congregation find new life—new life gained not by working harder or smarter, for the dead cannot work—but rather new life, *resurrection life,* given by God who raises the dead to life. *The Message,* Eugene Peterson's paraphrase of the Bible, reads, "You're blessed when you're at the end of your rope. With less of you there is more of God and his rule" (Matt. 5:3). Blessed is the congregation that has died, for now the possibility of being raised to life exists. A congregation at the end of its rope can receive the hope that God gives by the power of the Holy Spirit, foreseeing a life whose limits and nature are known only to God.

There Is Nothing New under the Sun

The author of Ecclesiastes observed that everything that has been will be again (Eccles. 1:9). The concerns about the church's future that have preoccupied ecclesiastical leaders for much of the past decade bear a striking resemblance to conversations that took place in the 1960s. An explosion of books on both sides of the Atlantic raised searching questions about what was wrong with the church, why it was failing to reach people, and how it had to change to become relevant to a modern world.

The theologian and thinker J. C. Hoekendijk, in his seminal work *The Church Inside Out,*[24] argued that the church needed to follow the example of Christ outlined in Philippians 2, emptying itself of power, position, and status, becoming a servant to the city, and walking in solidarity with the people. Self-emptying would allow the church to find new ways of being the church "in-situation"—in each unique context in which it found itself. Through small groups and the building of community to meet "human needs" through "genuine personal relationships," the church could address the deep longings of the society for spiritual communion. This vision for the church finds echoes in the writings of a number of contemporary church consultants, in particular Easum and Bandy. By rooting his argument in the self-emptying of Christ, Hoekendijk provides an important insight into what it means for the church to live its life following the example of Christ. However, he does not take this insight far enough, for Jesus Christ did not stop at the point of emptying himself to become a servant. He emptied himself to the point of death, even death on a cross (Phil. 2:7-8). The church too must die if it is going to experience the new life of resurrection.

In their 1964 work *Death and Birth of the Parish,* church historian and cultural observer Martin E. Marty and his coauthors recognized that death must precede new life. The dust jacket of the book depicts a phoenix rising out of flames. Aware of how hard "death" would sound to readers, Marty wrote, "The difficult jump for most people to make is to take these references to the individual sick [person] or sinner or the isolated Christian walking in newness of life and apply them to a sick and sinful church or a church walking in newness of life."[25] But it is precisely this connection that must be made if the members of the church are going to be ready for what God wants to do in and through the community of faith. The authors chose "birth" over "re-birth" or "renewal" in the book title to highlight that congregations must not simply go back to a previous model of parish life. "Birth" indicates something new—never-happened-before new. Surprisingly, the authors chose "birth" and not "resurrection." "Resurrection" carries with it not only the sense that the raised-to-life congregation is new, but also that its life is beyond the power of human beings to deliver. God alone can raise the dead.

Marty and his fellow authors provide important insights into the role consultants and experts play in the birth (resurrection) of the church. Recognizing that the motif of death must be extended to themselves, they write, "Our ideas, our proposals—to borrow the theme of the book—also have to 'die' in order to live."[26] This remarkable humility points to how loosely church consultants and congregational leaders must hold their own ideas and pronouncements about the future of the church. Marty goes on to note helpfully:

> God seems almost to have "written off" whole epochs and locations
> of the church in the past. . . . Perhaps our time is such an epoch and
> our place such a location. . . . But often out of a "written off" area
> in an unpromising time He has, through His servants and prophets,
> brought about newness and birth. If the social analysts awaken us to
> be ready for such devastation and birth, they will have filled a func-
> tion more important than that which they adopt when they bring in
> their prescriptions.[27]

The role of consultants is to mount the walls and to scan the horizon for signs of danger, sounding the warning when such danger is seen. They are called to be the prophets in the midst of the church. But as with the prophets of old, the only prescription they can offer is to invite the congregation humbly to surrender itself into the hands of the God who knows how to get out of the grave, and to say, "Not our will, but thine be done." Everything else consultants and critics declare is uncertain at best.

"There is nothing new under the sun" (Eccles. 1:9, cf. 1:10). Every idea has been thought before. Every solution has been proposed before, and most have been tried. So vapor-like were the ideas, no one remembers that they were tried before. When proposed again, the ideas sound new and exciting. But "[V]anity of vanities! All is vanity," proclaims the author in Ecclesiastes 1:2. The Hebrew word translated "vanity" could be better translated "vapor" or "mist." Wealth, material possessions, personal reputation, and even wisdom are but mist that will vanish and be forgotten. Not only is everything that human beings plan and do but mist; everything human beings plan and do also has been done before.

The author of Ecclesiastes notes a second challenge that confronts church leaders. God has "put a sense of past and future into [human beings'] minds, yet they cannot find out what God has done from the beginning to the end" (3:11). Humans, although aware of some of what has gone before, see the past only imperfectly. People are aware that there is a future, but it is unknowable. Church leaders are caught between an imperfectly known past and an unknowable future.

Is there then no source of lasting hope? The writer proclaims, "I know that whatever God does endures forever; nothing can be added to it, nor anything taken from it; God has done this, so that all should stand in awe before him" (Eccles. 3:14). Whatever is lasting is the result of God's working. God has also made a time for every activity under heaven, making everything beautiful in its time (3:11). There is a time to be born and a time to die (3:2). This is true of individuals, as it is of the institutions, such as congregations, that people establish. The life cycle of the local congregation includes birth and death. At any death, including the death of a congregation, there is weeping and mourning. But after the mourning come laughter and dancing (3:4). God acts to turn mourning into dancing, to turn funerals into celebrations of new life. God's action alone raises the dead. Any model of congregational renewal that fails to recognize this truth is vanity, a chasing after the wind.

CHAPTER 2

Congregations Confront
Their Mortality

Congregations are mortal. The proof of their mortality is evident from the church buildings that are now used as restaurants, theaters, community halls, or private residences. Sometimes a congregation is fortunate enough to sell its building to another; one congregation dies, and another is born. In other cases, a church forms, meeting in a member's living room or in the gym of the local school. The anticipated growth does not take place. The congregation dies, leaving no visible mark on the landscape; but the community of faith that gathered, calling the church its spiritual home, knows the pain and grief of the death. Congregations close their doors and are no more. They can die in many ways, however, and closing the doors is but one way to die. A community of faith may continue to function, meeting week by week, but with the vitality gone. Such churches need to die to their self-understanding so that a new, God-given understanding can arise. Congregations need to hold loosely to their vision so that they can be raised to a new vision.

St. Stephen's Church, caught in a demographic shift, faced this second kind of death. The families that built the residential subdivision and St. Stephen's forty years earlier had moved to retirement homes or warmer climates, and the new residents of the neighborhood were of an ethnic background different from that of the congregation's founders. St. Stephen's had a new mission field right on its doorstep. As new people from the neighborhood started attending, the church began to change. St. Stephen's slowly died to its Anglo traditions, including worship styles, decision-making patterns, and even the types of food available at congregational dinners, to welcome into its life those who now lived in the neighborhood. Some longtime members said, "This isn't my church anymore. The church I was once part of is no more." The congregation did not close its doors, but a death had taken place nonetheless. St. Stephen's died to one understanding of itself so that a new understanding could arise.

Advent Community Church was confronted with yet another kind of death. Advent Church's one Sunday-morning worship service no longer met the expectations of all within the congregation. As new subdivisions were built close to Advent, young families with children started coming. At first, longtime members were excited by what was happening. Over time, however, they realized that the new families expected contemporary worship music to be a regular part of the Sunday-morning service. The congregational leaders experimented with a number of ways to have one worship service that met everyone's desires, but they finally gave up. The only answer was two worship services within a single congregation. That was a difficult moment for Advent Church and its leaders. The congregation had to bury the belief that the only way it could be "one big happy family" was for everyone to worship together. While this death may not appear as dramatic as closing the doors, it was for many at Advent almost as painful. A new vocabulary needed to be learned—a vocabulary that assured attenders at both worship services that they were equally important to the life of the church. People needed to rethink their deeply held belief that "being equal" meant "being treated identically." Advent was a growing congregation, but that did not mean it did not have to die. It could not grow unless it was prepared to die so that a new pattern of life could emerge.

Significant research has explored the changes congregations need to make as they move from being pastoral-size churches (50-150 members) to becoming program-size churches (150-400 members), which is yet another form of death. The delegation of responsibility, the shifting role of the pastor, and the increasingly formal lines of reporting are the major changes in how a congregation functions. Changing from one way of being church to another is difficult. One pastor, confronted with the tasks involved in being "head of staff," said, "I need to go home and pray about whether I want to be in a church this size." The change from being a congregation of one size to becoming one of another size requires the death of one way of being church, so that new ways of being church can arise. Many family-size (0-50 members) and pastoral-size churches think they would like the "problems" of being program-size churches, but they have not recognized the practices that would need to die for that transition to happen.

Congregations should not fear death. They worship a God who knows how to get out of the grave. The death of a particular congregation is not the end of the story, as G. K. Chesterton notes: God is in the business of bringing miraculous new life to dead congregations. The death of a particular way of being church, or a particular understanding of the congregation, does not mean the church is lesser, for God is in the business of bringing new life out of the ashes of the old. That new life, however, comes only to congregations that are willing to die. Whereas some churches face death squarely, closing their doors and disbanding, others struggle, perhaps for decades, and still others give the appearance of thriving. Dying is a precondition to resurrection, nonetheless. All congregations, even ones that see themselves as healthy, need to be prepared to die, to take up their cross, so that God can make them alive.

Corporate Death in the Book of Judges

The biblical book of Judges provides a good jumping-off point for exploring how communities of faith die so that God can bring them to life. Three things recommend the book for our study. Judges portrays the people of Israel as a community. The community is not merely a backdrop against which the major characters of the book act. Rather, the people of Israel are collectively a character in Judges. The book provides a powerful antidote to the highly individualistic readings that dominate contemporary Western interpretations of the biblical material. Second, Judges knows nothing of leadership as discussed in the rarified atmosphere of today's leadership seminars. Instead leadership happens in the trenches, in the ebb and flow of real life. Painfully human, the judges provide today's church with a useful textbook on leadership. Judges makes a third truth clear: All human leaders are temporary. Life was taking place before the leader arrived, and things will happen after the leader is gone. Whether the leader's impact turns out to be long-term or short-term, the truth remains: the leader is limited. Reading Judges reminds a leader that he or she is but one in a succession of leaders God has called and will call.

Again and again in the book of Judges, the people of Israel cry out to Yahweh to be saved from one of the various groups oppressing them. In each instance the oppression took place for a significant period of time before Israel was prepared to ask God for help. The Israelites served King Eglon of Moab eighteen years before they had had enough (Judg. 3:14-15). The army of King Jabin with his general Sisera held sway for 20 years before "the Israelites cried out to the Lord for help" (4:3). It took seven years of Midianite oppression to bring the people of Israel to the point of acknowledging that they were unable to solve the problem themselves (6:7). The length of time it took the people to turn to God is significant. Things started going badly, and a few battles were lost, but that was not enough for the people to decide they needed help. Even after the land had been captured, they did not ask God to intervene. Years of oppression and slavery in their own land were required before the people cried out to God. Sometimes a single triggering event led the people out of denial to recognition of their true situation. At other times, the people turned to God only after a long and painful movement beyond denial. Significantly, not only the leaders—not just a small group of people with spiritual insight—but all of Israel joined in the appeal for help. Together, the people as a nation came to recognize their brokenness and the desperate nature of their situation.

The judges (prophets) called on Israel to look honestly at its situation, but the nation resisted doing that. The people of Israel wanted to be rid of the Midianites who had invaded the land, and so they prayed for help. God responded by calling Gideon to be a leader in Israel. First, God instructed Gideon to destroy the altar to Baal and to cut down the Asherah pole in his hometown. In their place, Gideon was to build an altar to Yahweh. Gideon did this—but at night, under the cover of darkness. When the townspeople awoke in the morning and saw what had happened, they were angry, demanding that Gideon be brought out so they could kill him. In a stroke of parental genius, Gideon's father, Joash, suggested that Baal defend himself. If Baal was a god, then Baal could certainly take care of Gideon, who was a mere human being. The people of the town, recognizing the logic of the argument, decided to let Baal defend himself. Thus Gideon's life was preserved (6:7-32). Gideon went on to lead a small band of 300 men armed with trumpets, torches, and clay pots, driving the Midianites out of Israel.

The incident with the Baal altar was a microcosm of a larger reality being lived out in all of Israel. The Israelites had cried out to Yahweh for help, it is true, but they wanted God's help to come in ways that fitted their notions of how God should save them. By destroying the Baal altar, Gideon confronted the people of the village, and Israel at large, with the reality that they were unprepared, as demonstrated by their attitudes and actions, to heed God's voice calling them to live as God's people. The villagers' anger, and by extension Israel's, was a sign of their unwillingness to admit they had no options left. Despite recognizing that they were in trouble, they were still unwilling to "let go and let God." The townspeople, and all of Israel, were called to stop putting limits on their commitment and to let God define the contours of the community's life of faith. Giving up control would mean trusting God to act and being prepared to follow God's instructions.

Reducing an army of 32,000 soldiers to a band of 300 and sending that tiny group against the enemy army, as God instructed Gideon to do, was complete foolishness in human terms. But letting go and letting God meant doing exactly that. The people of Israel had come to the point of saying, "Whatever God wills: nothing more, nothing less, nothing else."

Throughout the book of Judges, Israel tries to bargain with God. The most infamous of the attempted bargains was made by Jephthah and cost the life of his daughter, his only child. The neighboring Ammonites were in ascendancy and were threatening to take the Israelites' land east of the Jordan River. Israel was desperate, imploring God to do something. Yet instead of waiting for God to act, the Israelites took matters back into their own hands. They promised anyone who would drive out the Ammonites that the victorious general would be head over Gilead (10:6-18). The only person who could lead them successfully into battle was Jephthah, whom the leaders themselves had driven away (11:1-7). When Jephthah challenged the leaders of Gilead about this change of face, they replied, "Nevertheless, we have now turned back to you, so that you may go with us and fight with the Ammonites, and become head over us, over all the inhabitants of Gilead" (11:8). In striking a bargain with a savior, Israel and its leaders were striving to remain in control of the situation. Jephthah, filled with the spirit of God, became Israel's general and prepared for war. Almost as an aside, the reader is told of the fateful bargain Jephthah made with God: "[W]hoever comes out of the doors of my house to meet me, when I return victorious from the Ammonites, shall be the LORD's, to be offered up by me as a burnt offering" (11:30-31). Jephthah successfully led the army of Israel in battle and, upon returning home, was greeted first by his daughter. Fulfilling his vow to God, Jephthah offered her as a burnt offering to God.

Close reading of the text shows that the verses including Jephthah's vow are not necessary to the flow of the narrative, just as the vow was unnecessary to Jephthah's success.[1] God had blessed Jephthah, giving him the spirit of the Lord. Jephthah did not need anything more.

Nonetheless, Jephthah bargained with God, trying to control God, just as the leaders of Israel bargained with Jephthah to control what he would do. Strikingly, Jephthah's six years as leader of Gilead (following his victory) were troubled by conflict, as various groups within Israel made deals and counterdeals to protect or advance their interests. (Judg. 12:1-7) The story of Jephthah's judgeship is a cautionary tale about what can happen when human beings take things into their own hands: death occurs in ways that are unanticipated and undesired.

Denial, anger, and bargaining are evident in the story of Samson (Judg. 13-16). A special child from his conception, Samson struggled with God's call in his life. He denied the call to lead the people of Israel, living a life opposed to God's commands. His life was full of anger, most often directed at the Philistines, although his parents and animals also were targets of his wrath. Delilah's and Samson's relationship was filled with bargaining and coercion. Delilah deceived Samson into telling her the secret of his incredible strength, a secret she shared with fellow Philistines. When Samson was asleep, his head was shaved, and when awakened, he was unable to defend himself. He was captured and imprisoned by the Philistines, who put his eyes out. At the end of Samson's life, blinded and chained, he worked as a beast of burden grinding grain. Yet during the years of hard prison labor, a living death, his hair had grown back. As the Philistine leaders made sport of him, Samson quietly asked his guard that his hands be placed on the pillars holding up the building. Praying, "Lord God, remember me and strengthen me only this once," Samson brought down the house (16:28). "So those he killed at his death were more than those he had killed during his life" (16:30). While measuring a person's success by the number of people he kills is a particularly gruesome way of determining success, the narrator's point is that Samson was most used by God at this moment. Samson now understood that being used by God was the most important thing in life, even if it meant his death. Samson had denied God's call, acted in anger when confronted with the call, and sought to bargain it away. Finally, in his death, Samson accepted God's call.

The story of the people of Israel is the story of the people of God. Judges helps create a framework within which to understand God's working not only at that time, but at other times as well. Contemporary congregations are no different from the people of Israel. In the face of Gideon's indictment the people of Israel rejected the suggestion that they were somehow part of the problem; contemporary congregations likewise are often reluctant to admit that they have any responsibility for their decline. Unwilling to wait for God to act, the people of Israel made a deal to save themselves; contemporary congregations find that waiting on God takes too long and often turn to people or systems that promise congregational survival. When a church is in decline, and people in the pews are becoming worried, they, like the people of Israel, call out to God for help. But their prayers, often more implicitly than explicitly, define the nature of the help needed, setting out the limits within which God is to act. At some point on this journey a congregation stops putting limits on what God can do. The congregants, like Jesus in the garden, move from praying "Take this cup from us" to praying "Not our will but thine be done." The moment when a congregation learns "to let go and let God" is a profound one in its life, a moment that opens the door to the possibility of God's action. God in grace and mercy will bring hope and renewal. This is God's trustworthy promise.

This turning to God is not a once-and-for-all-time event. In Judges each successive generation of leaders needed to learn anew the hard truth that they could not be in control. In every community of faith, each generation of leaders must die to their goals and be reborn by the grace of God. Strikingly, the interval between crisis moments shrank the longer the Israelites were in the land. Following Ehud's judgeship, "the land had peace for eighty years" (3:30). Following Deborah's victory and with Gideon's rule, "the land had rest forty years" (5:31b; 8:28). Tola's judgeship was twenty-three years (10:2), Jephthah's six years (12:7).

Each generation of congregational leaders must discover for itself that the only way to lead is by letting God be God, dying to the desire to be in charge and being willing to follow God's lead. Further, the longer Israel was in the land of promise, the shorter was the rule of the judges. Might this point suggest that the longer a congregation exists, the shorter will be the time between congregational deaths and resurrections? Intuitively it seems likely that as the pace of change increases, culturally and congregationally, the life span of a given congregational leadership team shrinks. Even in a place where elders serve for a long time, perhaps even for life, the dreams and goals of the leadership team energize the congregation's life for a shorter period of time. And when a leadership team invites new people to join, that team is creating the opportunity, either intentionally or unintentionally, for a new understanding of church, a new congregational culture, to emerge. Each generation of leaders has to learn the truth that the church must die so that God can make it alive.

Giving up control so that God could bring new life and hope was the call issued to the people of Israel in the time of the Judges. The same call has gone out to the people of God throughout time. This call is not to be heard only by congregations in decline; it must be heeded by leaders of all congregations. Even churches that are apparently healthy must be willing to die to their goals, their plans, and their expectations, so that God can make them alive. The life of the church belongs not to the leaders of the congregation, and not even to the congregation itself. Life is a gift from God, and the congregation's life belongs to God alone.

Initial Congregational Responses to Decline

Just as Israel was a corporate entity with a personality and character, so also congregations have a personality and character. In what follows the reality of a church's corporate identity is taken seriously. Congregations respond to the same challenge in different ways, depending on their culture. As the congregational system becomes aware that the congregation is in significant decline, that this conditon is not just a blip on the radar screen, it tends to react in one of two ways: paralysis or frenetic action.

PARALYSIS

Paralysis can be driven by fear. Like a deer caught in the headlights, the congregation can be so mesmerized by what it believes is about to take place that it is unable to do anything to prevent the seemingly inevitable catastrophe. Fear can also paralyze a congregation when there is widespread belief among the members that "If we try to change anything, it could make things worse." This paralysis blocks any attempt to address what is happening. Congregations paralyzed by fear are sure that destruction is coming and that nothing will stop it. Moreover, a belief sneaks into the congregation's psyche that there is no hope. The discouragement that often comes with fear is palpable. The life of the congregation has the air of death row as the only event people anticipate is the announcement of the day of execution.

A consultant had been working with a congregation's leadership team to think through what initiatives the group could undertake. One group member was extremely negative about every initiative suggested. As the session continued, the consultant asked those gathered to project with realistic optimism where the congregation would be in five years. The member who had been so negative about any new initiative said, "We will be dead in five years." This man was so convinced that closure was inevitable that it was the most optimistic future he could envision. Despair can paralyze congregations.

At the other end of the spectrum, optimism can create paralysis as well. If fear blinds people to hope, optimism's rose-tinted glasses blind them to the truth of their situation. Congregations with long histories are particularly prone to see the present in optimistic terms. The conversation goes something like this: "This church has been around for more than one hundred years. There were tough times during the Depression, and the church survived. There were times when there was no money to pay the minister, but the church survived. The church has been through difficult times before, so just stop worrying." This kind of optimism leads to inaction and, more significantly, to unwillingness to take a serious look at what is happening in the church. The tough diagnosis laid out by those who have removed their rose-tinted lenses is ignored, or their view is portrayed as a negative and self-fulfilling prophecy.

In his best-selling book *Good to Great*, Jim Collins, former faculty member at the Stanford Graduate School of Business, proposes what he calls the Stockdale Paradox. Admiral Jim Stockdale was the highest-ranking United States military officer held in the "Hanoi Hilton" prisoner-of-war camp during the Vietnam War, being held from 1965 to 1973. Collins wanted to know why Stockdale survived and others did not. In conversation with Collins, Stockdale explained that POWs who saw no hope—who believed that there would never be an end to the torture and meager food, that freedom would never come—not unexpectedly died. More surprisingly, POWs who lived with optimism, persuading themselves that their imprisonment would be over by Christmas or by some other set date, only to experience the devastating reality of still being a POW past the date they had set—these also died. The prisoners who survived the "Hanoi Hilton" were those who held two seemingly opposite convictions simultaneously. They believed that some day they would be free, some day the terror would be over, *and* they were brutally honest about the nature of their situation. They recognized the truth about what they were facing, and they had hope that some day it would end.[2]

Churches are called to live within a paradox: facing with brutal honesty the reality of their situation, even when that appears to be a path leading to death, and living in hope that the God who knows how to get out of the grave will raise them up as well. Neither the paralysis of fear nor the paralysis of optimism is an option for communities of faith.

Frenetic Action

Frenetic action is another road congregations may take as they face their death. This chaotic activity is driven by a belief that the church is capable of stopping the decline, halting the slide to death. If the people of the congregation just pull together and work a bit harder, then the decline will cease. If everyone just digs a bit deeper into their pockets, the financial bleeding will be turned around. This activity is motivated by a commitment to the "run harder," "think faster," "be stronger" school of success. However, as Michael Jinkins of Austin Seminary writes: the church's "life does not depend ultimately upon . . . its executive competence, its technical expertise, its strategies, and its long-term planning."[3] Congregations put extraordinary amounts of energy into writing mission statements, devising long-term plans, and thinking through the strategies that will allow them to implement those plans. So committed do some congregations become to this work that they believe they are able through human ingenuity to stop the Grim Reaper's advance. Jinkins goes on to say, "Neither does [the church's] life depend ultimately upon its faithfulness, theological or moral."[4] For there is another form of frenetic activity that can overcome the church, the enforcement of theological purity. Such a discipline can be imposed by people at any point on the theological spectrum. Some contend that adherence to the creeds and confessions of the church will ensure the congregation's future health; others argue that without a commitment to complete inclusiveness, the church will have lost its way, being unable to speak to the culture; still others insist that only being a Bible-believing congregation can secure the church's future well-being. All of these approaches share a belief that human beings are able to act in ways that will guarantee the church's well-being.

Anticipating Congregational Death

Readers familiar with the stages of grief will have heard expressions of both the paralysis and the frenetic action common among congregations in decline as denials of death. Denying the possibility of death is a way of resisting loss. In their book *Leadership on the Line*, Ronald

Heifetz and Marty Linsky, both on the faculty of the John F. Kennedy School of Government at Harvard University, write about the leadership of organizations, institutions, communities, even nations. They state, "People do not resist change, per se. People resist loss."[5] Adaptive change—a change in habits, worldview, beliefs, self-understanding, or identity—involves loss. The old habits, worldview, or beliefs must die if they are to be replaced by a new self-understanding, identity, or way of being. So it is with a congregation; setting in motion a redevelopment or living into a new dream involves loss, the death of the old.

> Adaptive change stimulates resistance because it challenges people's habits, beliefs, and values. It asks them to take a loss, experience uncertainty, and even express disloyalty to people and cultures. Because adaptive change forces people to question and perhaps redefine aspects of their identity, it also challenges their sense of competence. Loss, disloyalty, and feeling incompetent: That's a lot to ask. No wonder people resist.[6]

When called upon to change, institutions, including congregations, resist the inevitable losses involved, seeking instead to retain their present way of life. In trying to hold onto their lives, churches become their own worst enemies. Only when a congregation is prepared to give up its life can new life come. In response to the threat of loss involved in the death of the congregation, members walk the path of grief—a path that includes anger, bargaining, and depression or despair.

ANGER

Asking a congregation to die so that new life can arise is asking members to lose their identity. People rebel when asked to die to a known and secure way of being church so that an unknown and uncertain way can be born. Breaking faith with the explicit, or more often implicit, promises made to previous generations is perceived as an act of disloyalty. Many members believe that they have been entrusted not only with the church but also with a particular way of being church, a way that must be passed on intact to the next generation. Not surprisingly, suggestions that a church is in decline and that the future of the congregation will require death are met with anger. That anger, however, is difficult for congregations to handle. Many congregational cultures have defined anger as an unacceptable emotion in the church. The members rarely express their anger directly, reverting instead to passive-aggressive approaches or simply repressing their anger until, when it finally erupts, it is directed at something completely unrelated to the real cause of the anger.

Anger's threatening storm clouds can be used to silence talk about the death of a congregation. The explosive nature of anger causes many people simply to clam up. Used in this way, anger becomes a way of denying a voice to those who want the church to face the hard reality of the future. An angry response does indicate that the talk of death has put into words concerns that other church members share. No longer able to deny to themselves the possibility of congregational death, some of those who respond in anger do not want the death talk to spread like wildfire. If others start talking this way, they worry, then people will start to believe the congregation is dying, and that will only make the situation worse.

Anger seeks someone to blame for the impending demise of the church. "Closing the stores on Sundays" and "banning hockey and baseball practices on Sunday morning," it is argued, would bring people back to church, and all would be well. This argument recognizes that the present culture is very different from that of the 1950s, and even that of the 1970s. Church members who became committed to their congregation in "the glory days" (the 1950s through the 1970s) are the ones who most often suggest banning softball tournaments on Sunday morning and the like. If the way things were "back then" was good enough at that time, it should certainly be good enough for people now. Changing societal patterns are blamed for the church's demise.

Shifting economic realities may also be blamed for congregational decline. Rural depopulation is often identified as the reason the twenty or thirty faithful people who gather Sunday by Sunday rattle around in a sanctuary built for two hundred or three hundred people. When the zinc mine in Johnson Mills shut down, everyone knew that there was going to be an exodus of people. As the churches in town struggled with dwindling resources and fewer people to help those who had been laid off, it was hard not to blame the multinational company that owned the mine for the churches' precarious futures.

Anger can be directed toward other people or groups within the congregation. The present leadership may be blamed for the decline, or some other group may be held responsible. Often an incident that produces a flashpoint for the anger has nothing to do with the long-term future of the congregation. Anger erupts over a seemingly insignificant matter, which when unpacked points to a deeper set of issues. Internal congregational fights alienate people on the edge of the church and those seeking to find a place to pursue their spiritual journey. Congregational conflict often drives away those under forty years of age. Members of this generation face enough conflict in their lives already, and they have no desire to take on additional conflict. The departure of this generation from a church provides the conflicting parties with the proof they need to blame the other for the church's demise. "If the opposition were not so intransigent, then those people would not have left; the opposition is destroying the church"—that becomes the oft-repeated refrain. Neither side in such a conflict is able to see its own anger and bitterness as a factor in people's departure from the church. Each side wants to be in control, believing the "other" cannot to be trusted with the church's future, for "they" will not be able to lead the congregation to health and wholeness.

No one could understand why Andrew had become so negative about everything; he wasn't his exuberant self. Then the light went on for Joanne, the Sunday school superintendent. Andrew had taught the junior-high class for ten years, but this year there was only one young person in the Sunday school between grades 7 and 9, so the decision had been made not to have a class. Andrew had been part of the conversation and had agreed with the decision, but that didn't mean Andrew was not hurting. There was no "safe" place for him to express his frustration and anger, so instead he criticized everyone else's plans. Congregational leaders take up their roles with high expectations of what might be. They come with hopes and dreams. The potential death of the church smashes those hopes and dreams, and anger becomes part of the grief response. Since the church is supposed to be "a nice place" where people do not get angry with each other, the anger often goes sideways, coming out in patterns of behavior that are sometimes hard for those outside the congregational system to recognize or understand. Ultimately the anger arises from the fear of losing the church.

BARGAINING

A third method congregations use to stay in control of their corporate life is bargaining, which happens when churches and their leaders seek to rope other people or groups into solving their problems. Congregations may try to bargain with denominational authorities, with God, and with the culture.

Church leaders may try to make a deal with the denominational authorities. Decisions made by the regional judicatory a decade or more ago are remembered and brought up as evidence of the governing body's culpability in the present situation. "If the governing body had just left this congregation alone, allowing us to do what we wanted," the argument goes, "everything would be OK right now." Since the diocese or presbytery or regional council is to blame for the present difficulty, it is also responsible for getting the church out of the mess. In this way the congregation seeks to abdicate its responsibility for the present crisis.

One of the bargains congregations try to strike is with God. In congregations where people are working hard and commitment is high, but where decline is seen to be deepening, leaders may begin to believe that there is a magic formula that will make the church grow. Workshops on ways to grow congregations are full of seekers hoping to find the life-saving program that will bring new life to the church. A visit to the resource collection of most congregations will reveal the various magic formulas that have been tried: The Forward Movement, Evangelism Explosion, Bring-a-Friend Day, Consecrated Stewards, and so on. These programs were not bad, nor were the underlying theological understandings wrong. Rather the variety of methods listed highlights the fact that the search for a program to save the church is not new. Seeking a new program or method is a regular fallback position for a church faced with its own possible demise. Even the theme of this book, that congregations need to die to be resurrected to new life, could be turned into a program promising to save the church. The search for the magic formula fits well with the increasingly technological understandings of how the church works. There are, it is claimed, surefire ways to grow a business, and so there must also be surefire ways to grow the church. The mysteriously wonderful workings of God in the world are codified and become predictable. Pushing the right button will make God act in a particular fashion. Bargaining with God is an attempt to control God.

Bargaining with the culture takes a number of forms. Some argue that nothing the church says or does should make the unchurched uncomfortable. Therefore, guitars and drums replace the organ, open-ended dramas replace expositional preaching, and inclusive language for people and God replaces exclusive language. The important question is: what is the motivation for these changes? If the changes are made to bring in more people to pay the bills, then the change is a form of bargaining with the culture. Calls for change that grow from a deep commitment to reach new people with the good news of a God who wants to transform their lives are to be celebrated. The difference between these two motivations is crucial.

Since money is a large concern for congregations, bargaining with the surrounding community to stay financially viable is tempting.

One of the primary things a congregation is called to do is worship God. This worship is for the benefit of both those who attend the service and those who do not. But a congregation may decide that its financial well-being is more important than its high calling to worship God, and may cancel its weekly worship service when the town fair is on, to run a fund-raising breakfast. In essence the church members are saying, "We are willing to give up one of our reasons for being so that we can make money to stay alive." A second calling of congregations is to serve their communities in the name of God. Yet a scan through small-town newspapers indicates that the only things some congregations advertise are fund-raisers, like rummage sales and fall suppers. Instead of serving the community, the church seeks to be maintained by those it should serve. A congregation that depends on the community for its financial well-being will find it difficult to fulfill its calling to be a prophetic voice in the midst of the community.

Bargaining is part of the complex pattern of mechanisms leaders and congregations use to control the church's future. Instead of letting go and letting God, they seek to maintain control of their future in their own hands. As should be clear by now, all these forms of death-defying activity are in fact unable to stop the inevitable movement toward death. Bargaining may breathe a little life into a nearly dead church, but it is not real life. Congregations find new life not by performing death-defying activity but through the power of God, who raises the dead to life.

Despair

Some congregations that know they are dying, and some that need to die to be given new life, still try to retain control to the very end. A core group within the congregation will do everything in its power to keep things the way they are. Nonetheless, a moment finally comes when even the last hangers-on admit that the congregation, or their vision of the congregation, is dead. This moment may come years after the congregation's vitality had ebbed away. All that is left is a shell of memory—memories of hundreds of children in Sunday school, fifty voices in the choir, young people's retreats, and support of mission endeavors overseas.

A disturbing pattern often emerges within the core group that fights to the end. Most of these people will not join another congregation, and if they do so, they will almost certainly not become deeply committed to that "other" church. Their Christian commitment evolved into a loyalty to a particular congregation, one that when tested by the fires of adversity became an intransigent never-say-die stance. Unwilling to die, these core members are unable to experience new life, resurrection life. Lay leaders of a closed congregation may say, "It will be a long time before I go to church again. How could God let the church, which has God's name on it, die?" Members who resist making the adaptive changes necessary for a congregation to move from pastoral-size to program-size church, for example, may leave the congregation they have served for so long, dropping out of all corporate faith activities. Leaders and congregational members may not have understood that the God who let the Son of God die on a cross, so that God's glory could be revealed, has no qualms about letting congregations die, *so that God's glory can be revealed.* Such a truth may come as a painful shock to leaders and members. The death of the congregation, either through closure or through a changing of congregational culture, often produces a crisis of faith for its members.

Key congregational players over time begin to realize that nothing they do, no amount of hard work, no greater level of giving, will ever be enough. The congregation they love and care for needs to die. This sad and often lonely realization is not the kind of thought people admit to their friends, let alone proclaim from the housetops. Leaders know that if they talk about the congregation's dying, they will be roundly criticized for not having enough faith. People in the pews sense that talking about the death of the church will lead to accusations of disloyalty, deeply hurting and maybe even insulting the congregational leadership. On a personal level it is painful to admit that the congregation is going to die. In this place children and grand-children were baptized, sons or daughters solemnized their wedding vows, communion was celebrated with others in the body of Christ. Acknowledging that the congregation is going to die is stating that a part of oneself is going to die. It is saying good-bye to an old friend.

With the realization that death is going to happen comes the lethargy of despair or depression. An exhaustion seeps into every part of congregational life. People talk about how tired they are, how they no longer have the energy to keep on doing everything they believe should be done. The truth that nothing can be done, in human terms, to save the church requires time to be absorbed. Grieving is tiring work that brings with it a physical, spiritual, and emotional exhaustion. This lethargy will be seen when congregational leaders who once were antagonists on every major issue have no energy to argue and debate. That people stop resisting the changes that will cause the death of the present way of being church is not to be interpreted as wholehearted agreement with the directions taken; rather, the lack of resistance is more likely to reflect acquiescence and surrender. Other congrega-tion members will pull back from many of their involvements in the church, saying they have too many things to do outside the church or that they need to spend more time with the family. These may be excellent reasons for curtailing one's involvements. However, when a number of people who have been highly involved start offering similar excuses, it is often a sign of congregational despair. By their actions members are saying, "Being part of the church is too painful right now." Or: "It hurts too much to see the congregation die." Still other congregants will put on a brave face, seeking to maintain a facade that all is well; yet a brittleness underlies this outward show. Periodi-cally, cracks appear, in the form of either tears or uncharacteristically angry outbursts. Having come to realize that congregational death is imminent, some members maintain a brave face to the very end.

As despair sets in, a point will come at which a key leader will say the fateful words "We are going to die" in a public context. This statement may not, however, be articulated so clearly. A congregational discussion takes place about the insurance on the church building, and a leader stands to say, "If the building burned down, we would not rebuild, so why would we pay the money for fire insurance?" This leader has not said the words "We are going to die," but the implication is clear: this church does not have a long-term future. This kind of blunt statement can have the effect of a bomb going off in a congregation. Some members will quietly agree with the speaker, thankful that they are not the only ones who have been thinking these thoughts. Other people, caught completely off guard by the utterance, will be shocked, even offended, that someone could say such a thing. Usually by the time someone has the courage to say publicly, "We are going to die," many within the congregation have begun to acknowledge that something is seriously wrong. Not everyone will have decided to head for the exits, but virtually everyone will agree that the future looks bleak.

Acknowledging a Congregation's Mortality

A congregation is more likely to reach the important moment of acknowledging its own mortality if it can do so with limited outside interference. The congregation that comes to understand its possible death through a process it has walked by itself has an experience dramatically different from the one that is told that it is going to be killed off by the actions of some regional denominational body. The first congregation, having had the opportunity to come to terms with its death and to experience the pain, will be better prepared to die so that it can be resurrected to new life. Being given the opportunity to confront this harsh reality in a way that fits the congregation's personality and style makes all the difference. The second congregation, having had no such opportunity, will perceive the pronouncement from the denomination as an attack from an outside enemy and will fight the coming execution. Outside agents may end a congregation's life when, for example, a diocese develops a strategic plan that deploys personnel only in churches with two hundred or more members, refusing to staff smaller congregations. Or a financial shortfall may cause denominational offices to cut off a grant to a seven-year-old congregation that cannot yet fully pay its bills, allowing the bank to seize the newly erected building and prompting the minister to find a new congregation to serve. In these situations, outsiders' attempts to arrange for a congregation's death will be rejected by the members.

There is a third way. A congregation that recognizes the need for change, one with leaders who understand that change is profoundly difficult, may begin to plan for its death so that new life can come. Many congregations recognize that they need to change but want to "change" without making any real changes to their life as a community of faith. Wise are the leaders who frame change as dying so that new life may come.

A dying congregation is more likely to find new life on the other side of the grave if it is led from within. This does not mean that outsiders have no role to play in the death and dying of a congregation. Rather, their involvement must be mediated through leaders who have *joined* the congregation.[7] *Joining* is more than being a member of the congregation; it means reaching a point at which the leader is emotionally, spiritually, and personally invested in the life of the congregation. Other members recognize this commitment to the congregation and may even say, "You know, Jill loves this church." If a congregational system is going to die so that it can be born anew, the church must have leaders, either clergy or lay, who have joined it. Only as leaders are prepared to die with the congregation, in the hope of being resurrected with it, will the church have the leadership resources needed to die so that it may be raised to life by the power of God. Joining a church that is dying, or that needs to die, is an emotionally costly venture, but the spiritually wise leader lives in the hope of a God who brings congregations out of the grave.

CHAPTER 3

Leading a Dying Congregation

Being a leader is dangerous. Laying out a vision is risky, for the vision will be critiqued and criticized. Ignored and discredited, leaders are often "cut down to size." They face attack. Leadership is an emotional roller coaster on which one is urged to remain "non-anxious." And these words describe leadership in relatively healthy contexts. Leading a dying congregation is not for the fainthearted. Leaders of dying congregations boldly proclaim that the way to life is through death, inviting the community of faith to test the truth of this statement.

Jeremiah: A Biblical Prophet

Jeremiah, the Old Testament prophet, lived during times that called for clear speech and firm faith. Loyal to Israel, Jeremiah courageously declared the coming destruction of the nation. Called by God to be a prophet, Jeremiah was warned that he would stand "against the whole land" (Jer. 1:18). Jeremiah plumbed the depths of God's words: he was banned from the temple, he faced death threats, and he was thrown into a dry well. The opinion makers—priests and government officials and kings—saw Jeremiah as a traitor. What other interpretation was possible, given Jeremiah's call to surrender to the enemy forces? The leaders sought to prevent Jeremiah from proclaiming the message he had received from God. As Jeremiah experienced external criticism and opposition, he had times of profound personal doubt: "Woe is me, my mother, that you ever bore me, a man of strife and contention to the whole land! . . . all of them curse me" (Jer. 15:10).

Two loves bolstered Jeremiah as he faced external opposition and internal self-doubt: a love for God and a love for the people of God. Jeremiah's love for God kept him faithful to God's call. The call, coming to Jeremiah as a young man, had seized his heart and would not let him go. Having been called, Jeremiah obeyed out of his deep love for God. Jeremiah also loved the people of God, Israel. Although Jeremiah said difficult things to the people, his love was evident in the tears he shed on their behalf. Jeremiah's love would not allow him to stand at an objective distance from the people of Israel; instead he was one with the people, suffering the same fate that many of them experienced.

Amid difficult circumstances, Jeremiah was not abandoned by God, for God gave people to help and support him: Baruch, Jeremiah's scribe; the Recabites, an Israelite clan who followed God's laws (Jer. 35:1-19); and Ebed-melech, the Ethiopian who arranged for Jeremiah's rescue from the dry well into which he had been thrown (Jer. 38:7-13). These individuals and others provided a network of encouragement as Jeremiah proclaimed the hard words God gave.

Jeremiah's message was not only one of doom and destruction. He pointed to a "future with hope," something God alone would bring (29:11). Israel would be in exile for seventy years. In exile, two generations would come and go, taking with them any confidence in Israel's ability to bring about a new future. By the third generation, the people would know that they were powerless to restore Israel. Jeremiah was a prophet of hope—not easy, cheap hope, but a hope that rested in what God would do. He proclaimed God's message in a letter to the exiles in Babylon, "Only when Babylon's seventy years are completed will I visit you, and I will fulfill to you my promise and bring you back to this place" (29:10). God would keep the promise, returning Israel to the land. This robust hope carried the people through seventy years, three generations of living by faith, not by sight.

Today's congregations are no more eager to hear that exile or death is the way to life than were the people of Israel. Death, be it the closure of the church, a change in worship style, or the decision to welcome a different ethnic group into positions of leadership, is painful. Congregations will use a variety of methods to dissuade leaders from proclaiming the hard message that death is the only way to find life. Leaders, however, are called to speak not only words of comfort but also prophetic words, even when those words are hard to speak and painful to hear. Although congregations will try to get leaders off message, they can resolve to stay on message.

Staying on Message in a Dying Congregation

In *Leadership on the Line,* Ronald Heifetz and Marty Linsky explore four ways that organizations attempt, often subtly, to stop leaders from bringing substantive change: *marginalization, diversion, attack,* and *seduction.*[1] Leaders need to be alert to these tactics. Congregations may use a number of techniques simultaneously to stop leaders whose message they do not want to hear. For example, diversion and seduction may be used together, making them hard to distinguish from each other.

Marginalization occurs when the congregation, or a part of it, succeeds in pushing the leader and the leader's influence to the edge of the congregation's life, where the talk of change can be safely contained. Angela had been the minister of Grain of Wheat Church for three years, and in that time she had come to the conviction that Grain of Wheat needed to make fundamental changes to its worship practices if the church was going to exist ten years in the future. Angela went to the elders and poured out her heart, suggesting that a group of people from Grain of Wheat concerned about this issue become part of a network of congregations that also wanted to change their worship style to reach those who were not part of a faith community. The elders agreed to send a group to a workshop to learn more about the network and how to change worship. Those who went to the event came back excited by what they had heard and seen; their excitement was evident as they reported their experience and learning to the rest of the elders. The other elders, somewhat cool to the new ideas, suggested that the group desiring to make changes should meet and produce a plan. Month after month, Angela and the group that wanted change spent hours together talking and thinking about what could happen at Grain of Wheat. When they presented reports to the elders, the elders would listen politely and then suggest that something else needed to be studied before they could give their approval. As time went by, Angela realized that the elders who had not attended the workshop did not want to make any changes, but they would never come out and say so directly. Those opposed to making changes were attempting to marginalize the agents of change, pushing their energy and excitement off to the side, so that they had no opportunity to influence the rest of the congregation. Through marginalizing the call to "come and die," congregations seek to silence those voices that urge adaptive change in congregational life.

Congregations are capable of distinguishing between the person and the vision, saying, "We love our pastor; she provides wonderful pastoral care and leads great worship—but we have no intention of making the changes she is suggesting." Pastoral leaders, on the other hand, tend to view the marginalizing of their vision as a limiting of their entire pastoral role. Pastoral leaders need to accept that they are seen as having at least two distinct roles in the life of the congregation: *pastor* (spiritual guide, preacher, caregiver) and *leader* (change agent, prophet). Pastoral leaders who fulfill their pastoral roles with integrity and ability will gradually earn the right to be change agents and prophets. When their vision is marginalized, pastoral leaders are wise to frame the vision in pastoral terms. In this way, the two roles are reconnected; and the pastoral role, which is much harder for congregations to marginalize, becomes the driving force for change.

Congregations are extraordinarily talented at *diverting* a leader from his or her agenda. A congregational leader may get buried in a host of issues and topics that are important to the people presenting them but that are largely peripheral to the leader's goals and dreams. Thus the leader is blocked from initiating a new vision. Mark had been called to be the senior minister at Eastminster Church, a multi-staff congregation. Worship attendance had been slipping for the past decade, and both Mark and most of the congregation were painfully aware that few young families with children were part of the worship life of the church. Mark, who had a gift for building relationships with young families, was sensitive to the changes Eastminster needed to make if younger families were to be included. Mark had high hopes for his ministry, believing that he had a mandate to bring change. But he found he had little time to use his gifts in reaching younger families, and almost no opportunity to deal with the systemic changes that were needed. His time was eaten up dealing with personality conflicts between staff members, endless committee meetings, and constant interruptions from members who came into the church office wanting to say "Hi" even though they had nothing substantive to discuss. Two years into his time at Eastminster, Mark looked back with disappointment over how little of what he had hoped to do had been accomplished. Eastminster had not really changed. But Mark was not sure where he would find the time and the energy to lead the change that was needed, because he was so busy that he fell into bed exhausted at the end of each day. Congregations do not want to get into the grave, and they will do everything they can to block changes to their identity and congregational culture. No one in the congregation is going to ask how well the leader is doing at getting the congregation to die to one way of being the church so that a new way of being church can be raised to life.

Leaders need to exercise discipline so that they are not diverted from calling for change. By taking control of their time, leaders can ensure that they remain focused on the vision. As leaders say no to various obligations, they free up time to spend on the more important role of being a leader (change agent, prophet). Blocking time into the weekly schedule for the tasks connected with being a leader is essential. Marking this time in the leader's planner as an "important meeting" makes it easier to say no to diversions. Secondly, leaders need to speak frequently of the truth that to die is to find new life—so frequently that the congregation begins to take on that vocabulary as its own. When this happens, the congregation is less likely to divert the pastoral leader from his or her accepted role.

Congregational leaders may have their call for change silenced by direct *attack*. By attacking the character of the leader who calls the congregation to die, those who oppose the congregation's death seek to stop any further steps in that direction. Attacking a leader's character is effective, because the leader will usually drop the new agenda and focus on self-defense. That is exactly what those launching the attack hope will happen. All leaders are open to character attack, because no leader is perfect. All leaders have limitations, failings, and things they do not do well. Leaders within faith communities also know that there is a God of grace who offers forgiveness and the opportunity to begin again. Leaders in faith communities can say, "Yes, I confess that is a failing of mine. By God's grace and with your prayers I will try to do better." Such an approach can defuse a character attack and allow the leader to get back on message. Leaders in faith communities should be somewhat immune to character attacks, because they know that the congregation's future is not their responsibility; it rests with God. Leaders therefore have a primary responsibility to God, not to the congregation. While this knowledge does not reduce the sting of the attack, it does place it in a different perspective. The question leaders need to ask is this: "Is this attack a sign from God that calls me to greater humility, or is this an attack against what God wants done?"

A fourth pattern used to stop leaders from implementing a new agenda is to *seduce* them with a different agenda. Jill came to Advent Church right out of seminary with lots of ideas and dreams for Advent. Among her hopes was to train laypeople to plan and lead worship services, and even to find one or two people who would be willing to learn how to preach. Jill decided that she would wait until the end of her second year at Advent to start this initiative, giving herself time to get to know the congregation and to identify which members had the gifts for this kind of work. When Jill raised her plan with the deacons for lay members to lead the prayers, they said, "Oh, but that would mean that we would not be having you lead us in prayer on Sunday, and you pray so beautifully. It just would not be the same if one of us did the prayers." Jill was flattered that people appreciated her worship leadership. But the deacons agreed that she could go ahead and try to find some people to be part of a worship planning group. As Jill approached people, she got the same kind of response: "We could not do as good a job as you do. We need to have you do this part of the life of the church." Again Jill was flattered, and decided to lower her expectations to just finding lay Scripture readers and giving up on the planning teams. Her vision had been sidelined. Congregations may block discussion of the congregation's death leading to new life by seducing their leaders into helping them remain unchanged.

Pastoral leaders are wise to ask themselves regularly, "To whom am I loyal?" Jesus said that human beings could not serve two masters. Pastoral leaders are called to serve God, a God who invites congregations to find new life by dying to their old way of being. Remembering where his or her first loyalty lies should reduce the pastoral leader's risk of being seduced by flattery.

Congregations often seek to silence the prophetic voices that call them to change. But pastoral leaders who understand their calling to be both pastor and leader recognize that they cannot surrender their prophetic calling, no matter how much marginalization, diversion, attack, and seduction they face.

Staying on message when people do not want to hear the message is difficult work. Congregational prophets are, like Jeremiah, given two gifts by the Holy Spirit to aid them in their calling. The first is the grace to be indifferent to everything but the will of God. When personal fears rise within the prophet, the Spirit brings a peace beyond all understanding. Congregational anxiety can pull leaders into serving the congregation's agenda (its survival), rather than being indifferent to all but God's will. The Spirit's peace not only addresses the leader's fears but also gives the prophet the words to speak to the anxieties of congregational members. The second gift the Spirit provides is spiritual friends. Leaders in dying congregations are lonely, especially when a leader begins to see the mystery of "dying to live" and other leadership team members do not. The friend that the Spirit provides may not be within the congregation, but that does not limit such a friend's ability to act as pastor and confessor to the congregational prophet.

Congregational Prophets

Congregational leaders are called to be prophets in their congregations. As one called from within the congregation, the prophet does not stand at a distance detached from the local faith community to which he or she speaks. Outside consultants or coaches may be helpful to a congregation, but the prophet is part of the congregation. Oddly enough, when it is "do or die" time for a hockey team in the playoffs, it is not unusual for the players to ask the coaching staff and sports psychologists to leave the room so that the team members, those who need to "do," can talk. Not only do the prophet's words matter; so does the prophet's love for and evident commitment to the congregation. Congregational prophets model what it means to die in hope, mourning the death of the congregation while holding fast to the hope of the resurrection. *Amateurs* in the original sense of the word, congregational prophets are "lovers" of the congregation of which they are a part.

Walking with the dying is always painful, and leading a dying congregation is no different. Prophetic leaders of dying congregations understand that the congregation's death is not about them; they are simply the individuals chosen by God "for just such a time as this" (Esther 4:14). That truth, however, does not eliminate the pain. In trying to avoid the pain, clergy may be tempted to professionalize their relationship with the congregation. Clergy remove themselves from the emotional pain of the dying church by developing a client relationship with the congregation. By regarding their role as that of providing a cluster of services to the client (congregation), clergy remain at some remove from the community of faith. Congregational prophets cannot allow themselves to professionalize their relationship with the members, to whom they are called to be passionate amateurs. Marshall McLuhan, the Canadian philosopher of the media and a devout Roman Catholic, put the distinction between amateurs and professionals neatly:

> The professional tends to classify and specialize, to accept uncritically the groundrules of the environment. The groundrules provided by the mass response of . . . colleagues serve as a pervasive environment of which [the professional] is contentedly . . . unaware. The "expert" is the [one] who stays put.[2]

Professionals function within a set of guidelines or accepted norms, which are usually the result of study and analysis. These ground rules offer safe places within which the professional can operate. The congregational prophet announcing that death precedes life and that only in accepting death will the congregation find new life is not playing it safe. Such a call is an invitation to a high-risk venture. The amateur trusts in God's love for the congregation, believing in the miraculous, unquantifiable power of God to raise the congregation to new life on the other side of death.

While the previous discussion was directed toward clergy, the intention is not to imply that only clergy can be congregational prophets. The prophetic voices may arise from any part of the congregation. Certainly clergy may be called to this role; so too may elders or deacons, but the Spirit of God also calls unexpected voices to speak with boldness the message of death's being the way to life. The faithful church member who rarely says anything but who stands at a congregational meeting and speaks from the heart may say more than the eloquent, frequently heard voices. A group of young people start to ask searching questions which the leadership group finds both energizing and frustrating—questions that push for new ways of being. A small group begins praying for new life in the church with unexpected results.

Congregational prophets are people who know that God can be trusted to bring life from death and hope from despair. Though they may wish they had not been given this task, these amateurs are driven by their love of God and their love of God's people to proclaim the shocking message that in dying, congregations can be born anew. They, like Jeremiah, know that proclaiming this message will require the courage and commitment to remain faithful to the message over the long term. As the congregation moves through the dying process, it will need to hear the message anew at each stage.

Leading Congregations through the Stages of Death

The rest of this chapter explores what congregational prophets, amateur leaders, either as solo prophetic voices or as members of leadership teams, need to say and affirm as they lead a dying congregation. The five stages of death and dying as identified by Elisabeth Kübler-Ross[3] serve as an organizing principle.

LEADERSHIP IN THE FACE OF DENIAL

Denial is the first way congregations seek to deflect the hard reality of congregational mortality. Those with the temerity to speak of death and dying are often ostracized and regarded as traitors. Prophetic leaders may be accused of being self-fulfilling prophets. If they would simply stop talking like this, skeptics and critics think, the whole problem would go away. The emotional and spiritual cost paid for continuing to speak can be high, particularly when the leader's family members are among those hurt by the prophet's words. Regularly examining their motives helps prophets ensure that their words are not driven by bitterness and anger at the treatment they receive. Prophets speak out of deep faith in God and a profound love for the congregation whose way of being they are challenging. Articulating the difficult truth, congregational prophets announce that death—even the death of this congregation—is something God allows.

Prophetic voices that insist there is a better life, a fuller life, a "more real reality" on the other side of the grave are hard to believe in a materially saturated culture. Life on this side of death is pretty good, many argue. Brian Moore, in his novel *No Other Life,* captures something of the hope and power of life after death when he writes, "The wake resumed, but all was changed: life had vanquished death. The corpse, stiff and silent at the table, would rejoin us one day in another, truer world."[4] Of that truer world the prophetic leader speaks. Church members will listen to the stories of that truer world, but few are ready to die to live that truer life. Congregations seek an easier way. Dying is too much.

Congregations reject the evidence that points to their terminal state. A decline in membership is not a sign of impending death; rather, the fringe of the congregation has vanished. Others simply reject all statistical evidence as irrelevant, for God has promised to be present with two or three. It will take time, sometimes a great deal of time, for the weight of the evidence fully to sink into the mind and heart of the congregation. The data should be presented clearly and concisely and left to do their work. The prophet does not need to persuade the congregation of the truth of the data. Statistics can ground congregants' nebulous fears in something tangible. Only the Spirit can open eyes to see what is happening.

Dying congregations often reject outside help. They are not sick; they do not need a doctor. In the early stages of dying, as congregations struggle with the possibility that they might die, asking for help is regarded as an admission of failure. Leaders may regard any offer of help as a slap in the face. It takes humility on the part of congregations to accept the help offered by regional denominational bodies. Denominational leaders as well need to act with humility in their approach to congregations in crisis. Lay leaders may reject help for themselves and yet recognize that their minister needs support and encouragement as the congregation faces "difficulties." In recognizing the challenges and stresses their minister experiences as leader of a congregation facing death, the members may come to realize that they can no longer deny the need to face some hard realities.

Wise leaders know that congregations need to hear stories of churches that have died and were raised to new life. Hearing other congregations' death-and-resurrection stories opens leaders to realizing that by denying the possibility of death, they may in fact be blocking their congregation's discovery of new life. Seeing death leading to life reduces the fear of death and makes leaders more willing to talk openly about the possibility.

LEADERSHIP IN THE FACE OF ANGER

A congregation may turn to *anger* and blame in response to the call to die to its way of being church. Anger frightens many leaders, and they need patience and grace to respond to it.

The massive shifts occurring in Western culture have pushed the church out of the public square. The sidelining of the church has taken place so rapidly that many faithful worshipers can remember a time when things were different. The "before" and the "now" stand in such contrast that some people within the church feel a deep-seated bitterness toward the culture for abandoning the church. These congregational members have, often unthinkingly, come to assume that the broader society is responsible for maintaining the church. Congregational prophets need to help people move past the anger they feel toward the wider culture by gently asking: How can we, as a community of faith, show love to a culture that seems to have rejected the church?

Anger may be directed not only outward but inward as well. Clergy may feel heat for not being able to stem the congregational decline. Congregational leaders may be criticized for being unwilling to change to keep up with the times, or alternatively they may be condemned for being too willing to change the deeply embedded traditions of the church. Some people will respond in anger toward seemingly insignificant incidents. It may be that the small item has become a lightning rod for anger that has been building for a while. The leader's first instinct may be to leave the anger well enough alone, hoping it will go away. Time does not heal anger, however. Time buries anger firmly in the psyche of the congregation. Unspoken undercurrents of tension and bitterness will cause people to reconsider their decision to be part of congregational life.

One way to start lancing the boil of anger is to hold a series of meetings at which the congregation is invited to tell its story. The congregation's unwritten history, built on the personal perceptions and assumptions church members hold about other people's motives and intentions, is far more important than what actually took place. Individuals tell meaning-making stories from their particular point of view, assuming that to be the only way of understanding the events described. Giving space for these individual stories to be told within a community context allows church members to hear one another's stories and to gain new insights into their own stories. The process is emotional, as old wounds come to light and difficult moments are relived. Yet if the storytelling is bathed in prayer, then healing and reconciliation can take place. This process cannot be rushed.

During the storytelling, anger may be directed toward various denominational bodies that are believed to have hurt the congregation. Clergy need to be self-censoring and to avoid communicating any defensiveness about these attacks on the denominational leaders. Letting the anger be voiced is more important than defending the denominational group that is being blamed. Congregations, however, cannot be allowed to end the storytelling having blamed the denominational structures alone for the death of the congregation. The person leading the storytelling time needs to highlight the truth that all parties share responsibility for both the good and the bad that are the life of any congregation. This shared responsibility can be noted with comments like, "Thank you for being so honest about your role" and "It sounds as though you appreciated those with whom you had disagreements." Prayers of confession and thanksgiving at the end of the storytelling become an opportunity to tell God the truth. Usually there are no completely innocent victims, nor any complete villains. The history of any local church is far too rich to be told in such simplistic terms.

Congregational leaders themselves may become the target of the blame game. In the midst of this seeming siege, leaders must remain focused on pointing to the new, resurrected life God holds out to all who are prepared to die. Sometimes the anger expressed by congregation members is not about the substance of what leaders say but rather about how it is said. Leaders can come across as cold and hard, even angry, when they talk about the congregation's impending death. Those prepared to show the pain they feel at the congregation's death will be more easily heard.

Although experiencing congregational anger directed at the leadership is uncomfortable for leaders, far more dangerous is the potential for them to be angry with the congregation. Prophetic leaders who recognize what can happen if the congregation dies may become frustrated with church members who have yet to grasp the reality that there is life beyond the grave: "Why don't they understand?" This frustration can flame into anger. Congregations are sensitive, instinctively knowing when leaders are angry with them. Prayer is the congregational prophet's access to the patience required in leading people who, like the disciples in the Gospel of Mark, do not understand that death leads to life.

Anger may be directed toward God. How could God allow this to happen? How could God allow my church to die? These questions are probably more troubling to the questioner than they are to the congregational prophet. Prophetic leaders know that God is big enough to handle these questions without their help. Congregants who have questions of God should be encouraged to ask their questions, to rail at God if need be. God can handle it and will still love them. Those asking questions of God can be gently reminded that the congregation is not theirs, that it belongs to God. God has the right to do anything God wants with the congregation. Ultimately a congregation will need to come to the point of saying, "Not our will but yours be done."

LEADERSHIP IN THE FACE OF BARGAINING

The *bargains* congregations are tempted to make are rarely between something good and something bad. More often the choice is to be made between two goods. Congregational prophets require wisdom to recognize which things are merely good to do, and which are the best to do.

Some church leaders and members attend workshop after workshop seeking miracle programs to save the church. When church members put their trust and hope in a scheme that promises to prevent congregational demise, congregational prophets are obliged to pull the congregation up short. The reasons for implementing a new program or plan must be carefully explored. If the program is seen as one more way to stave off death, a sign of commitment to persuade God to save the church, then prophetic leaders should ask some searching questions. Any belief that God can be bought off must be challenged. God is a God of grace who loves the church regardless of what people do. Ever greater commitment, ever more spectacular signs of discipleship will not cause God to bless the church. Congregations need to die so that they can be resurrected to new life—a life created not by the leaders, or by some magic formula, but rather by the miracle-working power of God, who knows the way out of the tomb.

Money's cold measure creates problems for clergy who depend on congregations to provide them with the necessities for keeping body and soul together. The congregation, after all, provides the resources that put food on the minister's table and clothes on the backs of the clergy family. If the congregation dies, the pastor will be out of a job. If a little bargaining with the culture will keep the church functioning a while longer, then bargaining is a good thing. The minister will get a paycheck for a couple of more years. It takes courage for clergy to tell a church that it is dying when they know that the congregation's death will most likely end their employment. Such an action, while true to the gospel, clearly runs counter to cultural, and possibly familial, expectations. Clergy, therefore, may be tempted to encourage financial decisions—such as using up the congregational endowment or emphasizing participation in fund-raising ventures over participation in weekly worship—that assist the congregation to hold onto life rather than challenge it to face the difficult reality of its terminal status.

LEADERSHIP IN THE FACE OF DESPAIR

Denial, anger, and *bargaining* are ways of maintaining control. They do not flow in a nicely ordered sequence within the life and death of a congregation; rather, they coexist in complex interconnection. Church members and even leaders grasp at these defenses as a way to retain control in a situation that is beyond control. Prophetic leaders gently but firmly say, "Control is not possible. The only way out is to give up control." The prophetic church leader points beyond the death of one way of being church to the promise of resurrection on the other side.

A time comes when congregation members move from trying to retain control to saying they see no hope for the future. They move to *despair.* People and leaders are tired and appear resigned to what is happening, but underneath hurt still throbs. People will want to know, "Where is God in all of this?" or "How can God allow this church to close?" Pointing toward another congregation, some will ask, "Why are we dying and they are not?" Not a new form of bargaining, these questions are rather attempts to understand the ambiguities of God's action in the life of congregations. The questions invite the congregational prophet "to come and mourn awhile" with the individual or group exploring the mysteries of life and death and life again.

Despair is a dark and hopeless place to live. Yet despair has something powerful to teach, as Eugene Peterson translates one of the

Beatitudes: "You're blessed when you feel you've lost what is most dear to you. Only then can you be embraced by the One most dear to you" (Matt. 5:5, *The Message*). Losing control of the church, recognizing that the future is not in the hands of the present congregation, opens the way for something far more important to take place. To let go is to let God.

LEADERSHIP IN THE FACE OF ACCEPTANCE

The art for leaders is to let the people experience the pain of despair long enough that the congregation actually understands that it is going to die. Congregational prophets let people view the corpse of the way the church was, so all can understand that bringing in a denominational crash cart or hooking up another program respirator will not bring the congregation back to life. The members must experience the loss. Leaders find it hard to allow this recognition to happen, for they believe it is their responsibility to protect the congregation from bad things and negative feelings. Witnessing the death of a congregation and feeling the agony of its loss is a bad thing, many leaders believe. However, only congregations that experience the grief of Holy Saturday can know the joy of new life's coming into the community of faith.

A congregational prophet, however, must not be so intent on the congregation's recognizing its impending death that he or she stops speaking of the hope of resurrection. It is of little value to the reign of God for congregations to recognize that they are dying unless they also know the promise that there is life on the other side of death. To paraphrase Paul, "If for this life only congregations have hoped in Christ, they are of all people most to be pitied" (see 1 Cor. 15:19). Leaders know that in the workings of God, death leads to life, and despair leads to hope. Both must be part of a congregational prophet's message.

There is life on the other side of death. The death of the congregation is not the end. In God's plan there is a future—not the future the congregation plans or envisions, but the plan God has in store, a plan more wonderful than anyone in the church could ever ask or think. Hope knows the terrible finality of death and, knowing that reality, points to the other side. Hope knows that God is in control and trusts God to bring about God's good plan. At the heart of God's plan is that death, all death, even congregational death, will be swallowed up in the victory of resurrection.

Dying: An Invitation to New Life

Ben Campbell Johnson and Andrew Dreitcer, both professors of spirituality, tell the story of a young minister who had a successful ministry, seeing more than three hundred people join his congregation in a three-year period, only to find himself suddenly fired by the elders. In his struggle to understand what had happened to him, the young minister came to seek counsel. After listening carefully to the story and sitting in silence the mentor said:

> I hear your pain. . . . But I must say that I'm grateful you've had this disorienting experience. . . . If you hadn't had this experience, you might have settled for being a handsome, successful, get-it-done sort of minister. . . . You have been driven so hard against the wall of your faith that you must decide if you believe in God, what you believe about God, and how you will relate to God. . . . My dear young friend, don't you see in this calamity, this pain and disillusionment, the evident invitation of God?[5]

Leaders of dying congregations see in the death of the congregation an invitation from God to trust God's ability to bring new life. They have a robust faith that has been refined in the fires of personal experience. They know the pain of loss—the loss of dreams, hopes, loved ones, and relationships—and they know the rugged truth that God is faithful even in the midst of loss. It is this fire-tested faith that makes the words of the congregational prophet so powerful. The words and the life have eloquence because they come from the prophet's having walked the road that he or she is inviting the congregation to walk. The congregational prophet is one who has been in the grave and knows that God can raise people and churches to life again.

The congregational prophet joins Jeremiah in being called "The Weeping Prophet." Death, any death, is painful, and the death of a church that has served the cause of Jesus Christ in a particular locality and in a particular way is something to be grieved. No congregational leader should ask for which congregation the bell tolls; it tolls for this very congregation. No congregation is an island. The death of any local church is a loss all congregations feel. Not to grieve such a loss is to deny the congregation's mission and the impact it had on the lives of the saints who were part of it. Leaders proclaim the message of "dying to live" against this backdrop. For the leader knows that, while the promise of resurrection is sure, the exact nature of the resurrected congregation and the timing of the resurrection are known only to God. The congregational prophet knows that resurrection will happen in God's time and in God's way.

CHAPTER 4

Spiritual Practices for Dying Congregations

"How can we sing the Lord's song in a dying congregation?" is the cry of congregations whose death appears imminent. In chapter 3 we explored some of the strategies and techniques leaders can use to help congregations face their death. In this chapter the focus moves to the hearts of the leader and the congregation: what spiritual traits can help congregations as they are dying?

Dying congregations join their lament to the lament of the people of Israel in exile in Babylon: "[T]here we sat down and there we wept when we remembered Zion" (Ps. 137:1). The glories of the past were remembered: the good times shared, the moments when God was clearly present and the future was full of hope and promise. These memories only added to the gloom and despair. The exiles hung up their harps and would not sing, for it was impossible to sing when Jerusalem and all that it represented was in ruins. The desolation of Jerusalem caused greater pain than any personal joy an Israelite might experience. The people had been marked forever; they would not be comforted or consoled. They would not again sing "one of the songs of Zion" (v. 3). "Dead congregations walking" are like this as well; they cannot, will not, sing. A powerful vortex of despair sweeps away congregations and their leaders. Everything is experienced through the pain of loss. Unable to hope, they are unable to believe that God might yet do a new thing.

Zechariah, John the Baptist's father, was unable as well to believe that God might do a new thing. His encounter with the angel Gabriel provides a cautionary tale for congregations awaiting resurrection (Luke 1:5-25). Luke recites Zechariah's spiritual pedigree: part of the priestly clan, as was his wife, Elizabeth; living a righteous life; and obeying God's commands. Members of the religious elite, Zechariah and Elizabeth knew what to do about the great sorrow of their lives: pray. That is exactly what they had done, praying many times, with great earnestness, for a child. They should have expected an answer from God, and in fact at the beginning they may have expected God to answer. As the years went by, their prayers for a child likely became less hopeful, more perfunctory. Past the time for having children, Zechariah and Elizabeth quietly accepted their childless state.

Gabriel appeared to Zechariah in the temple, bringing good news. In answer to his prayers, Zechariah heard, "Your wife Elizabeth will bear you a son, and you will name him John" (v. 13b). The angel went on to speak of the amazing things this child would do. But Zechariah was unable to hear of these great things, because he was stuck back at the promise that he was to be a father. He put his concern clearly: "How will I know that this is so? For I am an old man, and my wife is getting on in years" (v. 18). Zechariah, the priest, an intermediary between God and the people, was unable to believe God's amazing declaration that he was to have a son. In natural, physical terms, it was not possible. Hope had died, and the miracle Gabriel was talking of was too much. Zechariah was unable to believe that God could take his and his wife's barren bodies and perform a miracle, bringing new life.

Drained by being part of a dying congregation, members and leaders may come to believe that change is impossible. Doubt arises as to God's ability to do something new. Many within the church, not knowing what to suggest, say nothing; in a way they are "struck dumb." A few brave members suggest ideas that carry the hope of new life, only to hear others respond, "We tried that, and it didn't work." Prayers for the congregation's future become empty words, spoken with little conviction or power. Leaders do not believe that God can or will act. The denial of God's ability to bring new life to the church may never be expressed aloud, but the attitudes and actions of leaders and members declare their lack of faith.

Zechariah warns us how not to act, but Ezekiel is a model to be followed. The prophet, as we read in Ezekiel 37, was taken by the Spirit of the Lord to a valley of dry bones. Many people had died, and they had been dead a long time. God asked, "Mortal, can these bones live?" (v. 3). In human terms, Ezekiel knew the answer: No. Once the dead are dead, they are dead. Once nothing but bones are left, the person is not coming back to life. But because God had asked the question, there was another possibility. Ezekiel answered, "O Lord God, you know." This may appear a cagey answer: Ezekiel was making sure he did not say anything definitive to God, trying to keep his options open. Instead, given the whole tenor of the passage, we see that Ezekiel was stating the truth that nothing is impossible with God. If God wished to, God could bring new life to dry bones. God would decide what to do, and it was beyond Ezekiel's power even to guess what God might do.

Congregational leaders can emulate Ezekiel's humility. The bones were dry, and they had been awaiting resurrection a long time. Waiting is hard, for the longer the wait, the deeper the despair and the more distant the possibility of resurrection appears. But leaders do not know when God might act; that decision lies entirely in God's hands. Leaders are called to join Ezekiel in saying, "O Lord God, you know." Neither can leaders know what the newly raised-to-life congregation will look like. The shape of the new church is something God will determine. Congregational leaders cannot bring new life. No matter how much people point to this congregational leader or that pastoral leader as being the one who brought new life to a dying congregation, it is God who raises the church to life.

When Ezekiel made clear his belief that God alone knew whether the dry bones would live, God gave him a mission. Ezekiel was to prophesy to the bones, speaking the message God gave, a message of hope, a word of resurrection, a "thus saith the Lord" to the dry bones. As Ezekiel preached, God acted. Only God could put flesh and sinew on the dry bones, breathing into them the breath of life. Ezekiel was God's messenger to the people of Israel, who were saying, "Our bones are dried up, and our hope is lost; we are cut off completely" (v. 11). The people of Israel were the walking dead, without hope, without courage. God promised them, "I will put my spirit within you, and you shall live" (v. 14).

The uncontrollable nature of God's action is disconcerting. The bones rattling together, the flesh and skin appearing, the wind blowing—all were beyond Ezekiel's ability to influence. And turning a congregation's despair to hope, breathing new life into lifeless groups within the church—these are results present-day leaders cannot deliver either. New life, resurrection life, can be equally disconcerting to leaders and congregations. The nice, safe, well-trod paths of congregational life are suddenly thrown off-kilter by the shocking action of God. God makes the dead alive and expects congregations joyfully to join the chaos. The well-understood rule of nature—that life is followed by death—is turned on its head by God, who brings life out of death. Congregational leaders are to announce this upside-down reality to any who will listen, not because they have any ability to make the transformation happen, but simply because God has instructed them to speak of the overturned world God is building.

Dying congregations are only too aware of the dry-bones experience. The hope-sapping, joy-stealing destructiveness of death is palpable. Clergy have preached to the drying bones of the church as the pews became emptier and the faces of those attending turned more stoic. Congregational leaders have had their hearts broken trying everything in their power to turn the situation around, but nothing has stopped the slide. Church members have prayed fervently and worked tirelessly but have seen no fruit from all their labor. In this context, it seems foolish to speak of resurrection. The words sound hollow, ridiculous in the face of the overwhelming evidence of death. Words about resurrection bounce off the ear of the hearer, because all that can be heard is the death rattle of the congregation. But in the valley of dry bones of the dying congregation is precisely where leaders are called to speak of new life and where members are called to believe in resurrection.

Dealing with death is difficult, but dealing with the dead who are revived is beyond difficult—it is disconcerting, disorienting, beyond the safety of the predictable. Alan Lewis—at the time of his death, professor of theology at Austin Presbyterian Theological Seminary, Austin, Texas—noted, in writing about the theology of Holy Saturday, just how shattering is the new life that is promised:

> What frightens and frees us simultaneously about this new and alien kingdom of God which Jesus preached and told of is the simple fact that it is God's and not our own. That is a dark menace to the complacency and contentment of those who flourish under the kingdoms of this world; a shining vision of release and new beginnings to the victims of the present order; and perhaps also a mocking rebuke to the programs, projects, and pride of those who hope to create a new order by themselves.[1]

Lewis is right to highlight the double-edged reality of the new life Jesus preached. While the promised action of God is good news for all those who have come to realize they can do nothing to make the new life a reality in the world or in the local congregation, it is menacing to all those who still believe that the present structures are workable or can be adapted or restored by human ingenuity. New life cannot be constructed by human hands; resting in God's promise of resurrection requires humility. The church's spiritual disciplines provide a pattern for the practice of humility and offer hope to those who know that they are among the dead, the dying, and the denying.

Spiritual Practices for Dying and Denying Congregations

A brief reminder of what is meant by "dead congregations" is helpful at this point. That some congregations are dead is obvious to all: they have closed their doors; they no longer gather for worship; perhaps the place of worship has been sold or even leveled. Resurrection in these congregations deserves particular attention and will be addressed directly in chapter 5.

Those congregations that have closed their doors are not the only dead congregations. A second category of "dead" congregations includes those in which outwardly the activities of church continue, but internally the members see no future. Leaders have run out of ideas; the bag of tricks is empty. The organizational structure continues to bump along, but ever more slowly. People talk openly about when the end will come, how property will be dispersed, and what faith communities they might join. For some within the congregation it is a bleak and depressing time. Grief overhangs all they do and say. For others, those who have grasped the truth that death is the precursor to resurrection, here is a chance to live courageously, trusting in the graciousness of God.[2]

A third type of dead congregation is also in view: the one whose congregants are quite happily being the church: attendance is good, and the bills are being paid, but the spiritual fire has gone out. It is comfortable and has no desire to step out in faith, to take risks in mission and ministry. This congregation is dead as well, although it may continue to serve for years as a place where people gather for worship and fellowship. Yet over time the stench of death will become noticeable, even as people walk through the doors in reasonable numbers week after week.

PRAYER AND WORSHIP

What, then, is the dying congregation to do as it awaits resurrection? Two practices are central to the life of every church: prayer and worship. These practices open the door to the disconcerting action of God in the life of the dying or denying congregation.

Under the leadership of the legendary priest Peter Yorke, St. Peter's Roman Catholic Church, located in the Mission District of San Francisco, became the premiere Irish parish in San Francisco.[3] Yorke was succeeded by Ralph Hunt, who sharpened the congregation's Irish focus, adding the annual Yorke Memorial Mass in celebration of Yorke's ministry. The mass, begun on Palm Sunday 1927, became a fixture in the life of St. Peter's, and for the Irish Catholics of San Francisco. Through the 1940s Italian Catholics moving into the Mission started attending St. Peter's, so by 1950 it was an Irish congregation with an Italian flavor. Life was good at St. Peter's, even as the 1950s brought demographic changes to the Mission.

Hunt was replaced by the "100 percent Irish" Timothy Hennessey in 1950. With Hennessey came a Nicaraguan priest, Luis Almendares; he sought to reach the growing Hispanic community of the Mission, offering worship services along with confession and counseling in Spanish. His ministry led a growing number of Hispanics to connect with St. Peter's. Almendares was the first in a line of Spanish-speaking priests to work at St. Peter's.

In the early 1960s St. Peter's was blessed by a unique collection of priests. Timothy Hennessey did not understand his two young assistants, Jim Casey and John Petroni; but James Flynn, a priest working for the Archdiocese of San Francisco and living at the St. Peter's rectory, did. Flynn had Hennessey's respect and could speak Hennessey's language, and was able to explain the actions of the two assistants in ways Hennessey could accept. This acceptance in turn allowed Hennessey to explain their actions to the sometimes perturbed older Irish parishioners who did not understand why their church was changing.

By the mid-1960s, the 11 a.m. mass at St. Peter's was for the Spanish-speaking congregation, except on Palm Sunday, when the traditional Yorke Memorial Mass was held. During that service the predominantly Spanish-speaking congregation would listen dutifully through the English liturgy, gamely singing the English hymns. Then Casey would invite the congregation to conclude the celebration with a Spanish hymn, and "the congregation exploded into noisy singing, 'almost taking the roof off the church.'"[4] The old Irish congregation had died, and in its place a vibrant new Hispanic congregation had been born. As a number of the long-time Irish members of St. Peter's recognized, "all they had known was disappearing." One longtime parishioner even stated that the parish was "alien" to him. St. Peter's had changed.

Even as the Irish congregation of the 1930s and 1940s had prayed, "Thy will be done on earth as it is in heaven" week by week, the parishioners were unaware of what God's will might entail. Prayer and worship prepared St. Peter's to die to one understanding of itself so that the new life of the congregation could be revealed. Prayer and worship gave the congregation the spiritual resources to trust God to bring about new life. No cataclysmic moment of death took place, nor did an earth-shattering resurrection happen; yet the resurrection was no less miraculous for the gradual nature of its unveiling.

Prayer is communion with God, a communion that flows from this life through death, to life on the other side of death. Prayer lifts the congregation beyond itself, to recognize that life and death lie not in its hands but in God's hands. In prayer, the struggling congregation bears its anger, hurt, and despair, its moans of sorrow, to the only One who can handle them—God. It turns from reflecting on its terminal state to look to the God who knows how to get out of the grave. To walk through the drying bones of a congregation is to be driven to one's knees and to cry, "I believe; help my unbelief" (Mark 9:24). Walking this path leads to a deeper and more resilient faith. In prayer, the congregation learns to give its death to God, trusting that God desires for all to have life on the other side of death.

As congregations that believe everything is fine are praying for God's will to be done, they are opening themselves up to the subversive action of God, who takes seriously the words we pray. As the saying goes, "Be careful what you pray for; you might get it." The oft-repeated words burrow their way into the life of congregations, even of those faith communities that believe they have no reason to die.

The second essential discipline of dying congregations is worship. While prayer reminds the congregation who God is, worship tells the congregants who they are as a community: people created to glorify God and enjoy God forever. In worship the community of faith finds its deepest meaning and purpose as people who have been called by God to worship God. In worship, both the congregation corporately and the members individually most fully live out their humanness. As the congregation worships, it is drawn into the life of the people of God flowing across time and space and tradition. Worship here on earth is preparation for heaven. Congregational worship is preparation for the church's life on the other side of the grave as a resurrected congregation. Here the dying church touches practices that have been the heart of the church's life in the darkest hours of its history. In worship the congregation finds that even its impending death is given meaning and hope.

This worship will not always be joyful, for worship in a dying congregation will often be overlaid with a tone of lament. Some parts of North American culture are afraid of lament, preferring the "don't worry, be happy" approach to life. Churches have difficulty making room for lament in worship, often avoiding the reading of the Psalms of lament in public worship and rarely developing liturgical moments when lament can be voiced. If there is no lament for a dying congregation, then we have reason to question whether the congregation has truly been loved. The lament, however, will not be the lament of nostalgia. It will be lament over what has been lost because the local church no longer bears witness in its neighborhood and in the world. The loss of any community of faith should be mourned by the people of God. As the congregation laments in its worship, it does so with a profound trust that God hears and will respond. Out of the depths of its grief the congregation can sing "My Hope Is Built on Nothing Less" and "I Know that My Redeemer Lives" as expressions of its faith that even death cannot shake.

The disciplines of prayer and worship are not just for this life. They are part of our calling as people here on earth and in heaven. As congregations awaiting resurrection engage in the practices of prayer and worship, three spiritual traits will also be developed: *holy detachment, humble confidence,* and *the fear of the Lord.* These traits are essential spiritual attitudes for leaders and members seeking to live faithfully in the face of the hope-against-hopelessness message of resurrection in a dead congregation.

HOLY DETACHMENT

Congregational leaders need to develop *holy detachment,* holding loosely to the congregation, for it is not theirs, nor does it belong to the people who gather for prayer and worship, fellowship, and sharing. The church belongs to God, who called the congregation into being. Clergy and lay leaders must never forget that they are but stewards entrusted to oversee the congregation; they are not the owners. Called to do their best, leaders can claim no credit for any success in the life of the congregation. This understanding limits the ability of individuals to say, for example, "The changes in the order of worship were my idea, and I made them happen," and offers great freedom to leaders to give the life, death, and resurrection of the congregation to God, who holds the keys to life, death, and resurrection. Holy detachment frees congregants from the burden of claiming successes or justifying failures.

Exercising holy detachment is especially difficult for clergy. If the congregation dies and no longer has money to pay the bills, then the pastor is without a paycheck, a frightening prospect. Fearful of such an outcome, clergy may begin to overfunction, acting as though the church's success or failure depended on them. Pastors may also feel guilt about how much they are costing the congregation, and suspect that their continued presence is the cause of the financial difficulties. Clergy may listen to the inner voices that insinuate, "If you were a better minister, and able to bring more people into the church, this problem would go away." Still another reason clergy find holy detachment difficult has to do with their desire to be "successful." Some fear that having been the minister who "closed" a congregation will be a black mark against them, either affecting the way they are seen by colleagues or hampering their advancement within the career structures of the church. No matter how insistent clergy are that the church is not *about them,* their actions often speak of a very different understanding. As one familiar saying has it, "Ministers are people who on Sunday morning say it all depends on God's grace, and then the rest of the week work as though it all depended on their hard work." Only when clergy are able comfortably to claim their role as stewards will they be able to live with holy detachment in relationship to the congregation.

Holy detachment is not a call to irresponsibility. Leaders are stewards under orders, responsible to God for their actions. The glory and the blame, the praise and the accusations rest at the feet of God, who is the Lord of the church. Leaders thus have a calling higher than their responsibility to the congregation; they are accountable to God. Speaking of a minister's "serving a congregation" can be deceptive. A minister does not owe allegiance primarily to a congregation; a minister owes primary allegiance to God. A minister serves God from within the congregation. As people accountable to God, leaders are called to proclaim God's message, no matter how foolish the message may sound. Congregational leaders, both lay and ordained, are called to love people, and so they grieve the death of the congregation. But they have a higher love, a love for God. As lovers of God, they are prepared to be fools for Christ if that is what God calls them to be. No matter how ludicrous the words sound and the actions appear, leaders who practice holy detachment will proclaim the message of God's power to raise the dead, even the congregation that has died. The new life God gives to congregations often looks very different from their life prior to resurrection. Resurrection is not a matter of trimming expenses so that the doors stay open a little longer, nor is it the work of breathing life into the old church structures so that the congregation does what is needed to change. Part of holy detachment is being willing to let God raise the church up into the form God wants.

Woodbridge, once a rural community within easy driving distance of the bright lights of the big city, has over the past three decades been absorbed into the ever-expanding Toronto as a bedroom community.[5] Woodbridge Presbyterian Church has been in the community a long time. In the early 1960s, it had a thriving Sunday school with more than one hundred children enrolled and a membership of nearly two hundred adults. Thirty years later the church had not benefited from the community's population growth. The membership had fallen to forty-five, with half that number attending worship. The Sunday school had ceased to exist. The lay leaders were tired and discouraged by what they believed the future held for the congregation. A minister, David Sherbino, who was teaching full-time at a theological college, was invited to lead worship and to provide pastoral care on a part-time basis. Hiring someone part-time saved money, allowing the congregation to continue a bit longer; but the shift to part-time ministry did not inspire confidence as to the congregation's future.

Unwilling merely to provide Sunday worship and chaplaincy care, Sherbino asked the congregational leaders if they wished things were different and what they were prepared to do so that things could be different. The leaders responded that they were willing to try anything to see the congregation grow, and to help people grow in relationship with God. Sherbino identified five changes that would need to be made. These would become the direction for the resurrected ministry:

- A different approach to worship.
- Development of a small-group ministry.
- Implementation of evangelistic outreach events.
- Training and development of laypeople to do ministry.
- An emphasis on prayer in all that the congregation did.

The congregation was prepared to do all these things, along with investing $250,000 in repairing and remodeling the facility, so that it would be attractive to the new people who might come, especially those with children.

These changes required nothing less than a complete reorientation of the congregation's life. People had to give up one way of being the church, and to begin living in holy detachment, open to what God would do. One of the changes is that members no longer ask, "What has the church done for me lately?" Rather they ask, "What have I done for God recently?" This remarkable change took place quickly. The model of worship changed the Sunday after the people agreed to be a different kind of congregation. Ten years after the change 140 people are in worship weekly, and thirty children are enrolled in the Sunday school.

Remarkably, no one from the group that first sat down to talk about the dramatic changes needed has left the congregation. Of the eight elders who serve as the leadership team, four were part of the congregation before its death and resurrection. The story of the change, of the death of the old and the birth of the new, is well known within the congregation. Since some of the present leaders lived through the agony of impending death, the danger of forgetting what God has done is significantly reduced. They know what the church was like before, and they are prepared to die again if that is what it takes for the gospel message to continue to be proclaimed and lived out.

In 2005 the congregation had the opportunity to die again, so that a new kind of resurrection could take place. The remodeled building was sold, and the congregation moved into a new building, and in the process took on a new name, Cornerstone Community Church. While the small cluster of people who were part of the congregation before its resurrection have supported the move to the new building (having died once, they found it easier to do again), some of the people who had joined in the previous decade opposed the move to a new building. They were being asked to die so that new life in a new location might come; and not having experienced the earlier death and resurrection, they were not prepared to hold loosely to the life of the congregation. Living with holy detachment challenges congregations willingly to follow God's call, even the call to die.

With holy detachment congregational leaders announce that God is not limited to what human eyes can see or human minds understand: God invites congregations to die so that God can bring the dead to life again. In wonder at their own words, leaders of the dead congregation speak of the "God who raised him up," who is still in the business of raising up the dead and making the things that *are not* into things that *are*. Knowing that this belief is a scandal to the modern mind, leaders, ordained and lay, declare what they know to be true: God can make dry bones live.

HUMBLE CONFIDENCE

Congregations that have died are not dead; rather, they are congregations awaiting resurrection. With hope and confidence the leaders of these churches announce that God is in the business of raising the dead and breathing new life into dry bones. They proclaim, "God will raise us up, some day." God will certainly act, but on God's timetable. Jesus clearly stated, "No one knows the hour." Leaders must be tentative in all their statements about the future. The dead have no control over the future, no matter how much they may seek to control the action after they have left the stage called "life." The dead may be remembered, and people may refer to them; but the dead cannot speak for themselves and can make no prognostications about the future. The dead confidently await resurrection.

Michael Jinkins describes well the attitude underlying this waiting. Noting that he has "no idea what the church of the future would or could look like," Jinkins goes on to write, "I would hope that the reader would find what I have said very suspect if it appears that I am issuing a call for a new ecclesiology that will set at right all others, that will claim for itself a position of privilege above other theological perspectives."[6] Leaders who proclaim with confidence, as Jeremiah did, that restoration and renewal will take place also declare that they have no idea how or when that renewal, that resurrection, will take place. The leaders of the congregation are called to cast a vision of hope for this congregation, but they do so without presuming to describe how God will act or how the resurrected church will look. The resurrected congregation may not be in the image of the present one, nor will it be limited by the imaginations of the current members. Congregational members and leaders must not privilege those parts of the church's life they believe to be important by contending that those parts will survive. Likewise, it is presumptuous for leaders to pass judgment on those parts of church life that are problematic, jumping to the assumption that God will eliminate them from the resurrected church. Clergy, as they paint a picture of the future church, usually assume there will be a place for full-time paid clergy, privileging their own role. Leaders must guard against becoming definitive in their statements about what will or will not be part of the church of tomorrow. Attempting to delineate the character of the resurrected church in comparison with the recently deceased church is an exercise in futility, arrogance, and hubris. The congregation's new life will be given to it by God and God alone.

A vocabulary of "My God does this" or "My God cannot do that" can be heard on the lips of church people. Such language is dangerous, for it limits God to acting in ways that fit boxes defined by the speaker, a limited human being. Any attempt to limit what God can and cannot do is doomed to failure. God is in the business of breaking out of the boxes human beings so carefully construct to domesticate the Almighty. Never will God allow humans to tame or trivialize the Creator. Neither will God allow human beings, even if they are leaders in the church, to define what the church will or will not look like in the future. God has joyfully overturned the neatly defined models of church that have been constructed over time. Even the most cursory journey through church history reveals how God over and over again has sought to free the community of faith from the church human beings had constructed.

Is there then nothing that can be said about the church of the future? Jinkins is helpful in addressing this question when he writes, "These ecclesiologies must remain doggedly true to their historical rootedness, the canons of sacred texts and confessions, of narratives and community reinforced habits and practices that provide them with meaning and arise out of the particular forms of life observed in particular communities."[7] The newly resurrected church will have a life in continuity with the core life of the church through time, for the resurrected church is not cut off from its past. It has a past that is to be remembered and reflected upon. The congregation's past is recounted in the biblical narratives, the history of the people of God through time, and in the narratives of the local community of faith. The local church exists both as part of the flow of God's working in the world and as a body in a particular location in the world. While on the surface the resurrected congregation may look very different from what went before, it remains a church of Jesus Christ and will be recognizably such.

Some of the leaders at St. Andrew's Church in Flin Flon, Manitoba, a northern mining community, worried about what was going to happen at the congregation's annual meeting.[8] For forty years the congregation had been receiving a grant from the denomination that helped to fund the work and ministry of the church. But the writing was on the wall; the denomination was cutting back its grants, and the leaders at St. Andrew's were convinced that their grant would be cut. At the annual meeting they were going to take the bold step of inviting the congregation to vote that St. Andrew's not apply for a grant for the coming year. Some leaders fretted about the congregation's reaction.

The night of the annual meeting arrived, and the motion was introduced. A few logistical questions were asked, but there was an undercurrent of fearfulness in the room. No longer receiving the grant would be cutting off the lifeline. Not to apply for the grant meant giving up the safety of the known for the uncertainty of being a self-supporting congregation. Darlene got to her feet. She said, "I know we are scared, because we have never *not* had the grant. I don't know exactly what not having the grant will mean, but I do know that God will be with us. God was with us when we didn't have a minister for thirteen months, and we were not sure if we would ever get a minister. God was with us when all those people got transferred out of the community and we wondered if the church would survive. God will be with us if we go off of the grant." Unsure of what the future would hold, but confident that God would be with them, the members of St. Andrew's voted overwhelmingly to go off the grant. They had died to one way of being the church, choosing to let God show them another way of being the church.

Church leaders and members are called to remain confident in their proclamation of resurrection and the ability of God to raise up the congregation to new life, affirming that the spiritual core of its life will live again. But *when* that future life will come, and *how* the spiritual heritage of the congregation will be lived out in the raised-to-life congregation cannot be detailed. To speak of these things requires a humble confidence.

THE FEAR OF THE LORD

"The fear of the LORD is the beginning of wisdom" (Prov. 9:10); awe is required when dealing with God. A God who can raise the dead to life, who can take tired and discouraged people who have quit and transform them into a vibrant, excited, living community of faith, is a God in whose presence we stand in awe. Trivializing God, speaking of "the man upstairs," limiting God's scope of action, doubting God's ability to deal with the "big" things—these plague the church. Yet God remains the only One who can bring the dead to life again, and for that reason alone God should be revered. Just as the disciples in the boat on Lake Galilee were more afraid of this Jesus who could still the storm than they were of the storm itself (Mark 4:35-41), so the people of the congregation that has been raised to life again will be more in awe of the God who has raised them up than they were in fear of dying in the first place.

In her poem "Threatened with Resurrection" Julia Esquivel tears away thoughts of safely accommodating resurrection.[9] Esquivel was an elementary-school teacher in Guatemala until she was forced into exile. The hope that dominates the poem is not simplistic; rather, it is a hope refined in the fire of oppression and in the face of violence. The title raises a searching question for the reader. At first blush,

resurrection seems unthreatening. A threat is a bad thing, carrying
with it all manner of negative connotations. Resurrection is a good
thing, carrying with it signs of hope and renewal. How then could
resurrection be a threat?

Esquivel uses the common experience of sleeplessness to hold the
poem together:

> It isn't the noise in the streets
> that keeps us from resting, my friend . . .
> What keeps us from sleeping
> is that they have threatened us with Resurrection![10]

Parker Palmer, in his reflections on this poem, notes that Esquivel
never explicitly tells the reader who the "they" are who threaten resurrection. Is it the "demented gorillas" of the death squads?[11] That seems
unlikely, for the resurrection threatened is transformative and will "put
everything in its place." Rather it is the dead who are threatening the
sleepless with resurrection.

> They have threatened us with Resurrection
> because we have felt their inert bodies
> and their souls penetrate ours
> doubly fortified.[12]

The dead, the disappeared, threaten the living with resurrection,
for they have nothing else to wait for; they have nothing else to expect.
The only hope for the dead is resurrection—a hope so powerful that
it changes the living as well. In fact, it is more powerful than anything
else that confronts the living.

> They have threatened us with Resurrection,
> because they are more alive than ever before,
> because they transform our agonies,
> and fertilize our struggle,

because they pick us up when we fall,
and gird us like giants
before the fear of those demented gorillas.[13]

If resurrection is as powerful as Esquivel says it is, then it is more frightening than anything else in the world. For resurrection is greater than the final enemy, the greatest source of fear: death. Anything that can calm our hearts in the face of our greatest fears is more powerful than the fear itself. Whatever it is that can "pick us up when we fall" is a terrifying force. No wonder there is a noise that will not let the writer and the reader sleep. No wonder there is a power that stirs the tired, the discouraged, the dead; for resurrection is "the earthquake soon to come that will shake the world/and put everything in its place." This shaking will not be comfortable, for no matter how much the living mourn the loss of the dead, the fact remains: whirlwinds and earthquakes create enormous upheaval and rearrange the structures carefully made by human beings. The living who have walked the road Esquivel has walked know that they have no life as the living. The life they have is but a shadow of what real life should be. So the invitation is issued:

No, brother,
it is not the noise in the streets
which does not let us sleep.
Accompany us then on this vigil
and you will know what it is to dream!
You will know
how marvelous it is
to live threatened with Resurrection!
To dream awake,
to keep watch asleep,
to live while dying
and to already know oneself
resurrected![14]

The invitation is to dream not just of something new within this world; rather, it is to dream beyond the limits of this life, for the dreamer has been threatened with resurrection. Once the living know there is resurrection, once they have dealt with the fear of being raised to life again, then there is nothing to fear.

Esquivel never indicates who or what raises the dead to life. The Christian community, as it reads this poem, hears beyond the words of the poem the One responsible for the whirlwind and the earthquake called "Resurrection." In the face of that awesome power, all other dangers, all other threats, all other fears shrink to nothing. The God of all power, who can even bring the dead to life again, has been revealed. When this power is unleashed on and in the dead church, the sight is an awesome one, bringing a response of awe and wonder and praise.

The people of St. Paul's Church in Leaskdale, Ontario, a crossroads community northeast of Toronto, cannot believe what has happened to them.[15] The congregation was between ministers, and a consultant came to assist the leaders as they thought through the next steps. The consultant asked the leaders to project where they would be in two years and in five years if there were no changes. Everyone agreed that in five years the congregation would be a museum unless something different happened. The leaders committed themselves to being more welcoming of newcomers and to be open to change.

Both the minister of St. Paul's and the laypeople tell the rest of their story with wonder and awe. The rest of the story involves the congregation's growing to the point that two services were needed, and every inch of space in the building was used on Sundays, as 180 people worshiped at St. Paul's weekly. But God kept sending new people to the congregation, so they needed to move to a new site. They looked at a site that would have been sufficient for their needs, but the deal fell apart. Then a one hundred–acre plot became available. The church could build on part of the site, and the rest could be used to grow grain for shipment to people who did not have enough food. It was more than St. Paul's could ever have dreamed of. The new church building opened with seating for six hundred. Within three months it was full, and discussions had begun about adding a second service. As leaders from St. Paul's tell their story, they focus on the importance of prayer—falling to their knees before God, asking God to lead, to act, to give wisdom. In an ironic twist that only God could manage, the old church building has been sold to become a museum.

The leaders of the newly resurrected congregation live with a sense of awe that they have been honored to witness such an amazing event as the resurrection of a dead congregation. They know it was not *about them*, for it has everything to do with God's action. The leaders know that when the dead are dead, they are dead; in the raising up of the local church they have witnessed a miracle. Fear of the God who can do such things is a healthy and holy response to the miracle of God's action.

God Is Not Finished with Us Yet

Jesus Christ threatens the church with resurrection. The One who died, who has been made alive and who threatens to shake the dead congregation until everything is in its proper place, threatens to blow the wind of the Spirit through the church so that flesh and sinew and breath come onto the dry bones. This thought should both frighten and thrill any congregation awaiting resurrection. The memory of having been shaken in the earthquake of resurrection, of having the wind of the Spirit blow through the church, must be kept as a living story in the hearts and minds of the congregation. It is an awesome experience to fall into the hands of the living God, a God who can raise dead congregations to life again.

Keeping alive the story of the congregation's death and resurrection is important for two reasons. It reminds the leaders that it is God, not the leaders, who made the church alive. This resurrection did not happen as the result of any human action or ingenuity. The story is told with awe and wonder that God would do such an amazing thing for this congregation. The story of the congregation's death and resurrection is full of grace and surprise, fitting within the meta-narrative of God's action in the world. The congregation's resurrection story becomes its Exodus, its exile and return, pointing to the congregation's Pentecost. The telling and retelling of the story is not just a reminder of the past; it is also a vision for the future. Each generation of leaders needs to die. Each generation needs to learn, not just in people's heads through the hearing of the story but also in both personal and corporate reality, that they too must die if they want to find new life and new hope. Dying is the only way to new life. The story of the congregation's death and resurrection tells each generation of leaders that God is faithful and will raise up the congregation again, even when the doors have closed. The telling and retelling of the story becomes the narrative that teaches each successive group of leaders the practices of holy detachment, humble confidence, and the fear of the Lord. These death-and-resurrection stories become signs of God's faithfulness in the past and the promise of God's trustworthiness for the future.

CHAPTER 5

The Congregation
Raised from Death to Life

Being raised from death to life is a complete surprise, unexpected grace. So unexpected is it that we have difficulty imagining resurrection as the outcome of death. The dead do not come back to life; the dead are supposed to stay dead. Resurrection life is not merely the continuation of the same life; it is qualitatively different from the life that preceded death. In this chapter we move our attention to think about those congregations that have closed their doors, where the community of faith no longer gathers for worship, and ask how these churches might hear the promise of life on the other side of the grave.

The New Testament Resurrection Narratives

Even those who had been close to Jesus had difficulty recognizing the risen Jesus. Mary Magdalene mistook Jesus for the gardener (John 20:11-18). It has been suggested that she could not see clearly through her tears and therefore did not recognize him. This seems unlikely. Mary expected Jesus to be dead. The angels had asked her why she was weeping. Her reply made clear that she was looking for the body of the dead Jesus. Upon meeting the living, breathing Jesus, her mind refused to accept that Jesus had been raised to life. Even though there were similarities between the person she was talking to and the Jesus she had known, this man could not be Jesus, because Jesus was dead.

A story from my family illustrates how deeply rooted is the belief that the dead cannot come to life again. My grandfather, Howard Bush, was a soldier in the Canadian Army in World War I. While fighting in France, he was knocked out by a shrapnel burst. His unit kept moving, and he was left behind. His name appeared on that day's list of those killed in action. Staff at his hometown paper recognized the name and published a notice that he had been killed in action. His family knew he was alive, since they had received letters from him dated after the day upon which he was supposed to have been killed. When my grandfather was demobilized and returned home, people he met in the streets would call him "Ross," the name of his brother. The people in town saw the family resemblance and knew the man had to be a Bush; but Howard was dead, so this had to be Ross. The dead are assumed to be dead forever.

Failure to recognize the risen Christ is at the center of the story of the two followers on the road to Emmaus (Luke 24:13-35). On that Sunday-evening trip the travelers were not in tears; they were simply going home. Even though they spent a significant amount of time walking side by side with the risen Jesus (a seven-mile walk would have taken something over an hour and a half), they did not recognize him. How is that possible? Again, they did not expect the dead to come back to life. The fact that they were leaving Jerusalem and going home indicates that they had no expectation that anything unusual might happen. Being with Jesus had been wonderfully exciting. They had learned much. But now it was over; they would never see Jesus alive again. It was time to go back to the lives they had led before they met Jesus. But notice that they did not even comment to the stranger who was walking with them, "You look a lot like this Jesus we are talking about." They did not say to one another after they recognized Jesus in the breaking of the bread, "I knew there was something about him that was familiar." The way Jesus looked post-resurrection was different from the way he had looked before he went to the cross—different enough that he could not be recognized.

If Jesus did not look like himself physically, how then did people recognize that he was Jesus? Mary recognized him when he said her name. The two on the road to Emmaus finally recognized him when he blessed and broke the bread at the table. Thomas recognized him by the nail prints and spear mark (John 20:25-29). It was through actions—name spoken, bread broken, body touched—that Jesus was revealed as risen from the dead. He was recognized not because of his physical appearance but through his encounters with people. These encounters with the risen Jesus changed those who had contact with him; Mary, the two travelers, and Thomas could never again be the same. They too were resurrected—from despair to hope, from doubt to faith, from grief to joy.

Jesus was recognized as risen from the dead not because of physical similarities between his pre-resurrection and post-resurrection bodies but through the continuity of his actions after his resurrection with his ministry before his death. In the same way, the resurrected church will be recognized not because it has the same structure or outward appearance it had before it died, but rather because its ministry and actions will be consistent with the mission and ministry of the church throughout time and across geographical space. The mission and ministry may be lived out in various ways in different times and places, but the deep meaning will shine through. A congregation that has closed its doors may be raised to life as its dispersed members bring new energy to the congregations they join. Resurrection may happen as a new congregation with a new name, a different ministry style, of a different denomination, gathers to worship in a worship space that has been closed.

Congregations Raised to Life

Christians, both individually and corporately, live with the example of Jesus Christ. Congregations are called to follow the example of Jesus, entering the tomb to find themselves given new life. The new life of resurrection is granted to those congregations prepared to die. People who have witnessed the death of a church are surprised when it comes to life again. "Wasn't this church dead?" "Weren't you having meetings about closing the doors for the last time?" Such are the surprised comments from those who discover that the dead have been raised to life again. The skeptics wonder if it is possible that a dead church can find new life. Those within the congregation that has died and has been given new life know that the church has been raised to life by a power beyond themselves.

ALL SAINTS ANGLICAN CHURCH, TORONTO, ONTARIO

Established in 1872 to meet the worship needs of Anglicans on what was then the eastern edge of Toronto, All Saints Anglican Church had a remarkable ministry through the 1940s.[1] Stories were told of the 1,500 students in the Sunday school, the missionary in China supported entirely by the congregation, and other signs of health and effective ministry.

By the early 1960s, all of that was but a memory. Through the 1940s and 1950s, the middle-class members of the congregation had moved to the suburbs as the community demographics changed. Now All Saints was located on the edge of Toronto's "Skid Row," with the challenges such a location brings with it evident to all. All Saints was also on the skids, in a building that had seen better days and with a worshiping congregation that was both aging and shrinking with great speed. Through the efforts of a new rector, Norman Ellis, who was nothing if not blunt, All Saints began to look seriously at its future. Ellis had written to the bishop, "The opinion of the rector is that survival under the present terms is worse than death."

A number of plans were suggested, all of which involved significant changes to the All Saints building. One proposal was for All Saints to amalgamate with St. Bartholomew's Anglican Church, less than half a mile away, tearing down All Saints and selling the valuable property to provide an endowment for the future ministry of the amalgamated congregation. This proposal was rejected by the leaders of All Saints, who believed that the church had been called to a ministry in its present location. A second proposal suggested tearing down the parish hall and using the land to build a high-rise complex that would provide revenue for the running of All Saints. This proposal was rejected by diocesan officials, who questioned the feasibility of the business plan and worried that the diocese would be left carrying the mortgage.

Then came a proposal to join All Saints with St. Luke's United Church, located a block away—a plan that would allow ministry to continue in the neighborhood All Saints saw as its own. The sale of the All Saints property would fund a new inner-city ministry that would not require a building but would meet the people where they were. The diocesan and congregational leaders favored the proposal, but the congregation rejected it by the narrowest of margins. After this turn of events the bishop was given the power to disestablish All Saints at his discretion. For months the congregation and the rector waited for the inevitable, the decree from the bishop saying that All Saints was being closed. But the announcement never came.

Shortly after Ellis's arrival he had persuaded the lay leaders at All Saints to take steps to make the building more attractive. One of the most dramatic efforts was sandblasting the dingy exterior of the church. Suddenly the dark, hulking structure was returned to the yellow brick with red facings it had originally been. So dramatic was the change that many in the neighborhood could not believe it was the same building, and a streetcar passenger or two missed their stop, not recognizing the familiar landmark. As the congregation was waiting for its "execution," something unexpected began to happen: various groups that were seeking to make a difference in the community wanted to use the church as a base of operations. Suddenly the building, which had been such a burden, was a valuable and highly desired asset. The community that the church for so long had been trying to reach was now at the church's doors asking to enter.

For a congregation expecting death, the new life came as a surprise. The very burden that had been despised by some and worried over by many, the building, had become the congregation's strength. From this moment, All Saints built what would be most accurately described as a community-based ministry with self-help groups, daycare programming, and supports for the poor and downtrodden. Knowing the experience of rejection, the congregation was able to walk with the rejected.

It is true that All Saints did not close its doors; worship had not ceased to take place. Yet for all intents and purposes, the congregation was dead; all that needed to happen was for the bishop to issue the order, and the church would have been closed.

TOUCHING THE SCARS

The resurrected congregation is distinctly different from the church that existed before. So different is it that it can easily be mistaken for another church altogether. That does not mean that the resurrected church forgets it once was dead and now is unexpectedly alive. Though the story of the congregation's death may be painful to tell, the emotional difficulty of telling the story does not prevent its being told. In retelling its story, the resurrected church retraces its scars, showing them as signs of God's action in its midst. Just as Thomas would not believe until he had placed his fingers in the nail prints and his hand in Jesus's side, so many outside the resurrected church cannot believe that this is the dead congregation brought back to life until they see the scars. The resurrected church is unafraid of the story of its death because it knows the story does not end with death. Death was but a chapter in the longer story God is writing. Without death there can be no new life, and so the congregation tells the story of its death to give its resurrection context and meaning. By

speaking of its death, the congregation tells a story of resurrection
that offers hope, highlighting the grace of God. There is no other
explanation for what has occurred. No one could have predicted the
events and surprising turns that are part of the life of the raised-to-
life congregation. No one would set out a congregational plan that
looks like the one God has followed in the life of the resurrected
church. Anticipating the announcement of closure, locking the
doors for the last time, and disbanding the worshiping community
are not ways to grow the church. Those unexpected events, those
unpredictable turns, are evidence that this new life is not made by
human hands, but is the work of the God of hope who knows the
way out of the grave.

BETHEL FREE REFORMED CHURCH, WEST PERTH, ONTARIO

In 2003, Bethel Free Reformed Church[2] in West Perth, a forty-min-
ute drive north of London, Ontario, celebrated the one hundredth
anniversary of the church building in which the congregation worships. Located at the corner of a regional highway and a county side
road, the building was built by a Methodist (subsequently United
Church) congregation, which used it for sixty-five years, before the
United Church congregation was merged with another United Church
congregation a five-minute drive away. The merged congregation,
needing only one building, put the church at the crossroads up for
sale. The Free Reformed congregation purchased it in 1968 to be
its new place of worship. The new congregation could easily have
thought of itself as distinct from the United Church congregation
that had previously worshiped there. The members could have told
the story of their congregation in a way that ignored the sixty-five
years of history in that church building before their purchase of the
building. Instead, as was evident at the centenary celebration, the
Free Reformed congregation sees itself as continuing the worship of
the triune God in that location. To celebrate the building's milestone,

members and ministers of the congregation that had worshiped there
before 1968 were invited to return and to speak at the anniversary
worship service and the fellowship time following.

Even though a different congregation now worships in the building, using a different style of worship, both members of the former
congregation and members of the present one recognize a link between
the pre-1968 United Church parish and the current Free Reformed
community. How is such a link to be understood? Certainly the building serves as a tie. The speakers at the anniversary service, however,
implied a deeper continuity. While none of them used the language
of resurrection, theirs is in fact a death-and-resurrection story. One
congregation was merged into another and ceased to exist, and a new
congregation was born. The worship of the resurrected Jesus Christ
continues in that place.

By remembering the past—not just its own past but the whole
past worship of God in that location—the Free Reformed congregation is nurturing thankfulness and hope for the future. In remembering those who gathered for worship in that place before 1968, the
present congregation is able to recognize the gift of its situation. The
members are heirs of a worship heritage, heirs of a place dedicated to
worship for more than a hundred years. This story of God's faithfulness to the continuing witness to the gospel over time is a narrative
on which they can draw as a sign of hope. The congregation reminds
itself that God is in the business of ensuring that a witness to God's
action in the world will take place now and in the future, be that witness through the Free Reformed Church or some other congregation
that in its own time may use the building as its place of worship. The
story of the building engenders humility in the heart of present-day
congregational leaders.

The building's history blesses the congregation in a second way,
for it demands the telling and retelling of the story of how one congregation died and a new congregation was raised to life. The building
becomes a sign of death and resurrection, making it virtually impos-

sible for the congregation to forget that it is a congregation raised to life by a power beyond itself.

JOYFUL THANKS

The resurrected church is a thankful congregation. The new life is not a creation of the congregation; thus, the new life is not owned by or controlled by it. The new life is an unexpected gift, too wonderful to possess, too miraculous to cling to. It is to be held loosely, with open hands. Having come to understand that the new life is a gift, the resurrected congregation sees each new day as also being a gift. Gracious thankfulness is indelibly written on the life of the resurrected church.

The life the resurrected congregation lives is not its own. It is a gift from the God who knows the way out of the grave. Having taken the risk of dying, and having discovered what God can do, the resurrected congregation is prepared to risk its new life as the Spirit opens opportunities for mission and ministry. The measure used in determining whether to take up a new ministry challenge is no longer ensuring that the potential risks are low and the guarantee of success is high. Rather the question asked becomes, "Is the Spirit of God, who has given us our life, inviting us to take up our cross and follow in expectation of what God will do?" Having been dead and raised to life again, the congregation finds that little can frighten it. In boldness it is prepared to take risks for the God who gives new life.

FRIENDS COMMUNITY CHURCH, CARMAN, MANITOBA

Things were not going well at Gospel Light Church in Carman, an hour's drive southwest of Winnipeg.[3] "Internal difficulties" that no amount of wise counsel, conflict-resolution techniques, and external intervention seemed able to resolve reappeared regularly. But the Manitoba Mennonite Brethren Conference believed there was a need and an opportunity for a Mennonite congregation in the community. So the decision was made to close Gospel Light congregation and to start a new congregation in the near future in the same location with a new pastor. The Mission Board of the Mennonite Brethren would kill in order to make alive.

On April 30, 2003, Gospel Light congregation was closed. The congregation died without knowing what was coming next. The members would have to depend on the Spirit of God, who alone brings life to the church. An interim visitation pastor was brought in to provide pastoral care to "the dispersed congregation" until the new congregation was formed, providing some connection with what had gone before. In August 2003, the minister appointed by the Mennonite Mission Board to lead the "church restart" arrived in Carman and began work, "brainstorming, praying, gleaning ideas from other congregations and books, clarifying direction, meeting with the steering committee, and seeking God's mind in the development of this new congregation." An opening service of Friends Community Church took place January 4, 2004. The name came from John 15:15: "I do not call you servants any longer, . . . but I have called you friends." Using the former Gospel Light building, Friends Church has a very different style. People sit at tables during worship, and are encouraged to drink coffee or water during the service. "The setting also reminds us constantly of that future banquet that Jesus invites us to," noted Dale Warkentin, the "restart" minister. Friends Church has become a place where those who have difficulty fitting into the traditional models of church feel welcome and at home. The old structures and tensions are in the past; new life has allowed a freedom to move past previous difficulties and the constraints of "the way we have always done it."

Friends is a new congregation, but one with clear ties to its predecessor. The interim minister who had been visiting members of Gospel Light was involved in the opening service of Friends Church—a symbol of continuity between the old and the new. On the other hand, the "restart" minister arrived in town after Gospel Light had closed.

This mixing of new beginnings with clear reminders of what once was is typical of life in a congregation that has died and has been raised to life again. Friends Church cannot forget that once it was dead, but it has been made alive by the grace and mercy of God. At the opening service the interim visitation pastor read from John 15: "I am the vine, you are the branches." The church belongs to God; it is God alone who nurtures the branches to bear fruit.

KNOX PRESBYTERIAN CHURCH, AYTON, ONTARIO

Ayton is a crossroads community in the midst of farmland and wood-lots about a three-hour drive northwest of Toronto. Knox Presbyterian Church[4] was the smaller of two yoked congregations; the other, larger congregation was St. Andrew's, Hanover, about a ten-minute drive away. Knox's death took time. Finally a point was reached at which the members of the congregation recognized that the eighteen of them were tired of doing everything in the life of the church. They were tired of the constant struggle to keep the doors open; they were tired of knowing that if anything was going to happen, they would have to do it. After some soul-searching the congregation decided it would close the doors instead of amalgamating with St. Andrew's. This decision was made because it allowed the members of Knox the freedom to transfer their membership to the congregation of their choice, rather than having their membership automatically moved to St. Andrew's.

A year after the closure of Knox, St. Andrew's had grown by some forty people. True, seventeen of them were people from Knox who had chosen to make the ten-minute drive to Hanover, but what about the other twenty-three? Something surprising had happened. The tired, discouraged group of members from Ayton had found new energy and enthusiasm when they moved to St. Andrew's. No longer did they need to do everything; they could do those things for which they felt a passion. Able to offer their gifts and strengths in the places where they were employed to best advantage, the people from Ayton were not forced to fulfill roles they were not gifted for. Their enthusiasm in turn brought energy and excitement to the congregation in Hanover, which had plateaued and needed a new injection of life to take it to the next step. The new energy encouraged people at St. Andrew's to reach out to the community, and newcomers who had no previous connection with Knox or St. Andrew's became part of the congregation.

In its death Knox found new life, unexpected new life, at St. Andrew's. Only in the mystery of God would adding tired and discouraged members of one congregation to a congregation that was in need of new life and hope lead to the growth of the church. But the church has a God who brings new life out of death, hope out of discouragement, and joy out of sorrow.

Waiting on God's Timing

A problem lies behind everything that has been said so far in this chapter. Each of the stories recounted indicates that resurrection took place shortly after the congregation had closed its doors. Yet that is not the experience of all congregations that close their doors; some have been dead for a long time, and there are no signs that resurrection is about to take place.

A visit to the Cappadocia region of Turkey includes a tour of the ancient Christian sites. Such a tour takes in an ancient monastery with two chapels. In another part of Cappadocia a narrow river valley gives shelter to six small churches carved out of the steep walls of the valley. Worship has not taken place at the monastery or in these churches in over seven hundred years. No congregation in the district is the obvious heir of new life because of the death of these churches; there are no Christian congregations in the area.

God's timetable and our timetable are not the same: "[W]ith the Lord one day is like a thousand years, and a thousand years are like one day" (2 Pet. 3:8). The author goes on to say, "The Lord is not slow about his promise, as some think of slowness" (2 Pet. 3:9). The promise of the resurrection is a sure one; God can be trusted to bring new life. That new life, however, may not arrive until two or three or more generations have passed by the very dry bones of the congregation. The stories of congregations that have closed their doors and have been raised to new life become the fuel that keeps the flame of hope alive for those churches that have closed their doors and still await resurrection. Even after all who in this life were touched by the congregation have gone to their eternal reward, the promise of resurrection remains. Just as the church waits for its eschatological hope to be fulfilled, so dead congregations wait for their resurrection.

"Unless a Grain of Wheat"

These narratives tell the stories of a tiny fraction of the congregations that have experienced death and resurrection—God's plan for congregations and their leaders, a plan revealed in God's working with his people throughout time.

Congregational resurrections take place in as many ways as there are congregations that have been raised to life. The stories told here illustrate some of the ways God raises the church to new life. There is no suggestion here that these are the only ways God acts to raise local communities of faith from the grave. Checklists cannot be developed from these stories, giving people the tools to bring closed congregations to life again. The only pattern that links these stories is that all of these congregations died; three of those named in this chapter had closed their doors. And to all of them God gave new life in unexpected ways. I believe that thousands, even tens of thousands, of congregations can tell stories of death and resurrection. Such stories need to be told.

"[U]nless a grain of wheat falls into the ground and dies, it remains just a single grain; but if it dies, it bears much fruit" (John 12:24). This saying has been applied first and foremost to Jesus, the speaker of the words. Yet it is clear from what follows, "Those who love their life will lose it, and those who hate their life in this world will keep it for eternal life" (v. 25), that the application is much wider. These words apply to any follower of Jesus, to any collection of followers of Jesus. These words apply to the church. Unless a congregation dies, it cannot bear fruit. Only when a congregation dies does it realize that all the planting and all the watering are just so much planting and watering without the action of God giving the increase. The congregation cannot give itself life, cannot make growth happen, and cannot stem the slide to death. The ability to do all of those things belongs to God alone.

As it claims for itself the title "the body of Christ," the church declares its willingness to live out the paradigm established by Jesus, whose example was one that included death, even death on a cross. The church must therefore humble itself to the point of death, and then and only then will it find itself raised to life by the power of God. This death is not to be feared, for the church serves a God who knows the way out of the tomb. Death is a strange way to build success, but God's ways are not our ways. As the local community of faith gathers,

CHAPTER 6

Dying as the Way to Life

Jesus spoke challenging words to those who would follow him. "If any want to become my followers, let them deny themselves and take up their cross and follow me. For those who want to save their life will lose it, and those who lose their life for my sake, and for the sake of the gospel, will save it" (Mark 8:34-35). The cross had only one purpose in the ancient world: to kill. For only one reason would people carry a cross: they were on their way to death. When Jesus invited people to take up their cross, he was inviting them to die. This way is the path of discipleship. Yet the path of following Jesus did not end with his taking up the cross, for it is impossible to speak of the cross without speaking of the resurrection. To follow Jesus means following beyond the denial of self, beyond the cross, to the life that waits on the other side of the empty tomb. Holding on to life results in death; surrendering one's life by following Jesus leads to life.

Following someone is not a one-time event. The children's game "Follow the Leader" is not over in a couple of seconds. Following Jesus is for the long haul. Denying self and taking up the cross, which are part of following, are ongoing. They do not happen only once; they are repeated again and again in the life of the follower of Jesus.

It has been common practice to interpret this text in individual terms: "I am called to deny myself and to take up my cross and follow." While self-denial and personal cross-bearing are part of following Jesus, the New Revised Standard Version, in being inclusive of all human beings, enlarged the call. That is, by deciding to translate the first phrase to include the relative pronoun "if any want . . ." instead of "if any man wants . . . ," the translators of the NRSV are able to use the third person plural: "let them deny themselves and take up their cross." The text thereby takes on an added dimension: cross-bearing and following Jesus are not activities done only by individuals; they are also a community venture. The congregation is invited to take up the cross, giving up its life so that it can find new life in following Jesus. Just as individuals are called to follow over the long haul, so too are congregations. Local communities of faith are to deny themselves regularly, take up their cross constantly, and follow Jesus, knowing that this is the only way to life.

The Rule of St. Benedict captures this unlikely path to hope when it instructs its followers: "Yearn for everlasting life with holy desire. Day by day remind yourself that you are going to die."[1] Life is found through a recognition that one will die. All human beings and everything that humans build will eventually die; resurrected life, life on the other side of the grave, is a miraculous gift of God's grace. Week by week as the community of faith gathers for worship, it is reminded that it will die and that new life will come about only as the surprising outcome of that death.

Knox Presbyterian Church, Bayfield, Ontario

Knox Presbyterian Church in Bayfield, Ontario, a community of seven hundred on the shores of Lake Huron, was on its last legs.[2] The congregation had been a second or third point in any number of yoked pastoral charges over the previous thirty years, but by the late 1960s, Bayfield was viewed as a liability by the other Presbyterian congregations in the area. No single-point congregation or yoked congregation was interested in sharing its minister with Bayfield on Sundays. Bayfield was on its own and was unable to support a minister on even a part-time basis. Leaders within the presbytery (the regional judicatory) assumed that the congregation would quietly go away and fade to black, without the presbytery's having to act to put it out of its misery. But one more meeting had to be scheduled, at which time the members of the congregation would be told that no one wanted them. The minister sent to deliver the harsh message was not prepared just to say, "Go away; we don't want you." Instead he told the members they had a choice. They could close the doors, or they could try a radically different approach—becoming a summer student mission charge.

Being a summer student mission charge would mean having a student minister for sixteen or seventeen weeks each summer and being closed the rest of the year. The congregation would not have a minister of its own. Ministry would continue, but it would look very different from the kind of congregational life the members had had. Far more responsibility would devolve to the lay leaders in the congregation, whose role would change from supporting the minister to becoming mentors and guides to the students who were learning what ministry was really like.

The congregation chose to take the risk of doing church in this new way. "What did we have to lose?" is the most common explanation congregation members give when asked why they opted for this radically new approach to ministry. The story of that momentous meeting is part of the church's living memory, for it is regularly retold. Congregation members know that once they were dead, but now they have new life. The keepers of the story within the congregation clearly state that the risk was worth it. For more than thirty years the congregation played an important role in training clergy for full-time ministry. One member wrote an article titled "The *Other* Seminary" for the denominational magazine, highlighting the ways the congregation had helped train clergy. I am a product of the Knox, Bayfield Seminary, having been the summer student in 1988.

Knox became a congregation that trained clergy only because it was prepared to die to one way of doing church, so that it could be reborn into a new model of church. Expectations about being a year-round church had to go and be replaced by a new view of church life.

Lay leaders had to be willing to step into new roles, taking risks they would never have been willing to do in the previous ministry model. Further, the congregation had to give up its perception that only ordained people could lead worship and preach, and instead deal with a string of students who were in the process of finding their preaching voices. All of this was possible only because the congregation had died. By remembering that they had died and had been resurrected into this new way of being church, the members were able to see each new student, no matter what idiosyncrasies he or she brought to the summer internship, as a gift. The strange and risky ideas students brought with them could be tried, because, as members viewed the situation, nothing could be worse than what Knox had already experienced, that it had died. This is not to say that Knox, Bayfield, was not discriminating in the kinds of ministry it would do or in the kinds of preaching it found acceptable. In fact, the congregation developed a clear understanding of its ministry and a clear way of evaluating the quality of the preaching it heard, based on whether the kingdom of God was advanced and on whether Jesus was lifted up. The resurrected church knows that the quality of ministry is to be measured not by whether it maintains the tradition of the congregation but by whether it points to the risen Jesus Christ.

After more than thirty years of training students to be ministers, Knox faced an unexpected crisis early in the new millennium. Demographic changes among those attending theological college meant that fewer students were willing or able to move to Bayfield for four months. What was Knox to do if its reason for being was evaporating? A second shift, this one in Bayfield, had been taking place at the same time. A growing number of people were choosing to retire to Bayfield, increasing the year-round population. Through the latter half of the 1990s, Knox had used the services of a retired minister in the area to supplement the summer ministry. The congregation took a break from weekly worship during the cold months of January and February. The retired minister preached in March, April, and early May. The summer student arrived in May to lead the services and to do pastoral work through until early September. And then the retired minister led worship and preached until Christmas. By the winter of 2001-2002 the leaders at Knox realized that the two changes were forcing them to rethink the model of ministry. Although giving up the training and mentoring of students for ministry was painful, the opportunity to have a year-round ministry in their community was heard as a call from God. That winter, 2001-2002, I played a role in leading Knox to die to one way of being church so that a new way could emerge. The congregation grieved the ending of the summer student ministry and with some fears moved toward the challenges entailed in year-round ministry. Those members who had lived through Knox's previous death and resurrection reminded the congregation that God had raised up the church before and was capable of doing it again.

The two deaths Knox has died are somewhat different. The risk in dying to the previous way of being church so that the summer student ministry could be born was accepted relatively easily, since the only other option on the table was closing the doors. Dying to the summer ministry so that year-round ministry could happen was more challenging. There appeared to be more to lose: a successful ministry of training students was going to be ended, and a year-round minister who would not be leaving at the end of the summer was being called. Dying is never easy, but sometimes saying good-bye to what has been is easier when it is clear that death is inevitable. Dying to what has been a fruitful ministry, one that still appears to be doing well, often feels more risky. Yet the call to take up the cross and follow Jesus comes not just to congregations that recognize their terminal status; it comes to all congregations, even those that believe they are healthy.

Habits of Congregations

Wise congregations develop habits that help them to integrate denying self, cross-bearing, and following Jesus into the essence of their identity. These congregations understand that dying to find new life is not a one-time event; rather, it is a way of being the church. Among the habits developed are wonder, remembering, and risk taking.

WONDER

In the play *The Cotton Patch Gospel,* the risen Jesus appears to his disciples and says with joyful surprise, "It worked!"[3] He trusted that God could raise the dead to life, yet believing that God could do it and actually taking the step of dying were not the same thing. Moving from the theoretical to the actual raised the bar. Jesus appeared to his disciples in wonder and amazement at the surprising grace of God that raises even the dead to life. The new life was all gift, all grace, all God's.

The congregation that has died and has been raised to life again knows the same surprise. No matter how deep the faith, no matter how profound the trust in God, taking the step of dying—be that dying to one way of being the church or actually closing the doors—is a moment filled with fear and uncertainty. The congregation echoes the words of the man with the son who suffered from seizures: "I believe, help my unbelief" (Mark 9:24). Notice that this verse appears less than a chapter after Jesus' call to his followers to come and die. The author of Mark may be inviting readers to recognize just how difficult trusting God to raise the dead is. Resurrection is a surprise—a moment of unexpected joy as mourning is turned to dancing. From now on, the life the congregation lives is no longer its own, for the life it lives is the gracious gift of God. The congregation did nothing to earn this new life; it did nothing to call the new life into being. All the congregation can do is say in shocked amazement and joyful thanks to God, "It worked!"

The raised-to-life congregation exudes a sense of wonder at what has happened to it. Leaders quietly say, "I need to pinch myself to find out if I am just dreaming." Longtime church members shake their heads in disbelief, saying, "I never thought I would see the church alive again." This amazement affects every aspect of the church's life. Despair becomes hope, for within the congregation a spirit of anticipation prevails: "If God could raise the church to life again, what else might God do?" The wonder at what God has done creates gratitude. Recognizing their life together as a gift, the congregation moves away from an attitude of entitlement to one of thankfulness.

Since the congregation's life is not its own, there is no room for pride or self-congratulation with this new life. Congregational leaders tell the story of the church in self-effacing ways. The result is as surprising to the teller of the story as it is to the hearer. The storytellers are clear: the new life did not result from planning and hard work. The leaders of the congregation are not to be credited with the results; instead the One responsible for the transformation is God. When leaders are asked, "What did you do that created the change?" the stumbling answer is, "Nothing—all we did was die. God did the rest."

Wonder, gratitude, and humility are among the traits that grow in a congregation that has been raised from death to life. These traits renew every aspect of congregational life. Worship is changed as wonder and gratitude fill the church in its singing, praying, and listening for God's voice. Decision making is changed as humility embeds itself in the heart of the congregation. The congregation that has died and has been raised to life again is changed; it is no longer the same.

REMEMBERING

Sadly, over time congregations sometimes forget that the life they are living is a gift. They begin to think that somehow they have brought this life into being by their own ability and hard work. As the philosopher and poet George Santayana wrote, "Those who cannot remember the past are condemned to repeat it." Forgetting where the congregation's life came from is a prescription for going through the process again.

In the book of Revelation, the risen Christ accuses the church in Ephesus of abandoning its first love. The cure for abandoning something, forgetting its importance, is to remember. The Christians in Ephesus are called to remember the way things used to be, recalling the things they used to do. Remembering is central to congregations that have died and have been raised to life again. In remembering, these congregations rekindle the fires of wonder and gratitude, stoking the embers, so that the surprising gift of the congregation's life burns bright in the heart of the congregation.

Congregations that have died and have been raised to new life are also called to remember—remember the way things were before: to remember the despair and hopelessness, to remember the inability of human leaders to bring substantive change, to remember that nothing could stop the slide toward death. Although it may seem unnecessarily painful to remember the way things were before the new life came, it is only in remembering the death of the congregation that the new life finds a context. The move to call the Sunday before Easter "Passion Sunday" makes clear this requirement. The good news of Easter has real power only when it is seen against the background of the events of the Passion. To ensure that church members, who may not attend Good Friday services, appreciate that background story, the lectionary offers readings for Passion Sunday focusing on the events surrounding the death of Jesus on the cross. In the same way, the new life the once-dead congregation is living makes sense only against the backdrop of the congregation's reality prior to resurrection. Understanding the congregation's earlier life is as important for those that have had to make radical changes in their corporate life without closing the doors as it is for those that have in fact closed their doors. In remembering, congregations affirm that the life they live is not their own, but rather is a surprising gift.

The stories congregations tell about themselves are important. Churches that have been raised to life tell and retell the story of their death and of God's surprising action in bringing them to life. In telling this story, the congregation reminds itself of who it is and communicates to newcomers the central pieces of its identity. The story becomes so well known that all that is required is for a church member to make a brief reference to the story and everyone within the congregation knows what is being said. Admittedly, the easy use of such shorthand is frustrating for those who do not know the story, yet it illustrates how deeply rooted the story has become in the life of the congregation.

In the telling and retelling of the congregation's story, the church finds its story fitting into the larger story of God's working in the world. The purpose of remembering is not just to celebrate what God has done. A congregation's spiritual life becomes brittle if it is built entirely on the past. The congregation remembers so as to strengthen its faith in the present and into the future. The story must remain flexible enough that it can be understood as contemporary and fresh by successive groups of leaders and members.

Familiarity can breed contempt, and the routine repetition of the story may cause some people to stop hearing it. In my experience at least, those who did not experience the congregation's death and resurrection in the first place are most likely to become immune to the story's power. Those members who have experienced the death of the congregation once and have seen the amazing grace of God at work in bringing new life are more likely to be prepared to die again. As these people listen to the congregation's story, they remember the faithfulness of God in raising the dead to life again. If God did that once, then certainly God can do it twice, and a third time, and even more times.

TAKING RISKS

Congregations are often far too afraid to takes risks in their corporate lives, fearing that their actions may jeopardize the church's life. Leaders may be hesitant to change the style of worship for fear of upsetting people. Communities of faith may worry that by developing programs to reach people in need, they will be regarded as being too political. Clergy may choose not to speak clearly on issues, believing that forthright speech will alienate donors. Such fears hold congregations trapped, unable to move outside safe paths. Playing it safe leads, as Jesus noted, to losing one's life.

The congregation that has died and has been raised to life knows there is something worse than dying, and that is *not living*. Jim Elliot, missionary to the Auca people in South America whose martyrdom with four of his colleagues was the subject of the movie *End of the Spear*, understood this truth.[4] He wrote, "He is no fool who gives what he cannot keep to gain what he cannot lose." God does not call congregations to play it safe but rather to take risks. There is more at stake than survival. Responding to God's call to serve a broken world, living out the love of God for "the least of these," speaking prophetic truth, are things that trump the desire to survive. All of them may bring the congregation into places where it may be called to risk its life.

Serving God pulls congregations out of the controlled environment of the predictable and safe and into the chaotic world of the unforeseeable and risky. A small group from St. Matthew's, a downtown church, wanted to help the homeless, so its members decided to serve a hot supper once a week to the handful of people who frequented the front steps of St. Matthew's. This simple act evolved unexpectedly into an "Out of the Cold" program. Once a week, three or four dozen homeless people come to St. Matthew's for supper, fellowship, and a place to sleep. The program has its risks, as some from St. Matthew's have made clear. Some homeless person could go out of control and do damage to the building, or hurt another guest or one of the volunteers. Providing food and shelter has financial implications, stretching St. Matthew's limited resources. A few longtime members indicated that they felt unsafe coming to the church when "those people" were around. While the leaders of St. Matthew's acknowledge that initiatives like "Out of the Cold" threaten the congregation's life materially and financially, they know that the deeper threat is spiritual. If St. Matthew's is unwilling to risk its life in mission and ministry, it will discover that in trying to protect itself from harm it has already forfeited its life.

Congregations that understand their life is not their own, that know God can and will bring new life to dead churches, are often prepared to take risks that threaten their life. The argument in favor of taking risks goes something like this: "If we take such-and-such an action, what is the worst thing that could happen to the congregation? It is true that it might die, but God is in the business of raising dead congregations to life again." Even death, the greatest of all threats, should not be frightening to the church.

Risks come in all shapes and sizes. Often the issues involved with the big risks are so obvious that leaders are clear about the right decisions to make. Leaders may be frightened by the implications of the decisions they make, but they know what they need to decide. At times, smaller risks are more difficult to assess. What is at stake is not always clear. Yet the congregation that has died and has been given new life knows that it cannot play it safe; it must be open to taking risks.

Jim, the pastor of St. Chad's Church, was worried about what Muriel Stuart would think. The deacons had decided to make significant changes to the worship experience at St. Chad's by introducing a worship band, complete with drums and guitars. Jim went to visit Muriel, the ninety-five-year-old matriarch of the congregation, to explain carefully what was happening and why. Muriel laughed at his fear and said, "As a child, I came to this church in my father's sled. He had a loaded gun across his lap to shoot at any bears that might come out of the woods. In my lifetime, I have experienced two world wars, seen people walk on the moon, and lived through the communications revolution. And you are worried about my reaction to having guitars play during the worship service?" Jim left Muriel's home having learned an important lesson: many congregation members are far more willing to take risks than leaders recognize.

Congregations choosing to take risks rather than seeking their own survival are blessed. Such congregations are led by people who recognize that their obligation is not to maintain an institution but rather to follow the risky path of responding to God's call. Risk taking joins remembering and wonder as the habits of congregations that have died and have been born again. These three habits function to keep alive the truth that congregations are called to die not only once but a number of times as they seek to live out the call of God in their corporate life.

Dying as a Pattern for Congregational Life

The people of Israel in Judges experienced a series of deaths and rebirths. Over the centuries the church has experienced numerous declines and deaths, only to find itself raised to life again each time. Congregations experience the same reality, dying and being reborn not just once but again and again.

Death and rebirth form the pattern of congregational life. Leaders and members within communities of faith that have died and have been reborn know that the present way of being church, and even the congregation itself, will not last forever. Understanding that the life and practices of the church will not remain unchanged, they are open to the transformation that comes from dying. Congregations that have died are not naive about the pain involved in dying, for they have already walked the road that leads to the grave. But they also know that the new life God offers on the other side is more than worth the suffering. In humble confidence they take up their cross, knowing that the God who invites them to die is able to raise them to life again, as he has done in the past.

As the elders' meeting was drawing to a close, Stephen introduced a piece of new business. He moved that Sherwood Park Church build an elevator to make the church more accessible. Lynne, the minister of Sherwood Park Church, was chairing the meeting. She knew it would take time to come to a good decision about installing an elevator and that the discussion could be divisive in the small congregation. She thanked Stephen for his motion and asked if the elders were prepared to enter into a discernment process about the proposed elevator. The elders agreed, setting aside their next meeting for that work.

As the elders gathered the next month, they noticed that a cross had been placed on the table in the center of the meeting space. As part of the task of discernment, Lynne gave each elder an index card, inviting them all to write down those things that were stopping them from hearing what the Spirit of God might be saying. They were not to share what they wrote with anyone else. One elder wrote, "We don't have the money to do this; we will be broke." Another wrote, "The other churches in the neighborhood have elevators; therefore we should get one." Stephen wrote, "I may soon be in a wheelchair, and I want to still be able to come to church." Unsure of the response she might get, Lynne then invited those who were willing to place the cards at the foot of the cross as a sign that that they were willing to die to those personal opinions or reservations, choosing to follow God's lead wherever that might take them. In less than a minute all of the elders had placed their cards at the foot of the cross. The discernment process continued, but the tension that had been present earlier was gone. The elders had laid aside their personal agendas and concerns to listen for God speaking in the words of others, in the silences between those words, and in their own hearts.

Congregational leaders ask themselves, "What do I need to die to so that new life can come? What am I doing that is preventing death from taking place, and is therefore stopping new life from arising?" Through spiritual reflection and a process of discernment, leaders can identify places in their lives where, by clinging to a process, an initiative, or a personal dream, they are blocking a death from taking place. Having identified what they are holding onto, leaders are called to renounce those things, reaching a point of becoming indifferent to everything but the will of God. Leaders are called to put into practice what they preach, modeling for the congregation dying so that new life can come. These leaders understand that what God is calling the church to do and to be may require the leaders to surrender their vision and their expectations so that God's gift of new life can be revealed. As leaders are prepared to renounce their goals and dreams so that God's vision can be seen, congregational members will be more willing to let go of the things they are holding onto that are blocking the new life of resurrection.

Congregations that know death and rebirth are part of God's plan ask, "Where in the life of the congregation are there signs of death? Where do we see the denial, anger, bargaining, and despair that accompany the dying process?" These are areas to pay attention to, because they may be the areas where new life will bloom. Precisely in those places where death has taken hold is the hope of renewal the greatest. In the stone-cold tomb, death had taken hold, yet the empty tomb stands as the boldest sign of God's action.

In dying and in being born to new life, the local community of faith finds its story connecting to the larger story of God's action in the world. The power at work to raise Jesus from the dead is revealed anew as congregations are raised from death to life. By the grace of God, the community of faith is given reason to hope in even the most

Epilogue

Late one afternoon a couple of weeks after her realization that both she and her congregation, St. John's Church, needed to die to their goals and agendas if they were going to find new life, the Rev. Sarah Turner was visiting Joanne Peterson, an elder at St. John's. Sarah and Joanne were sitting on Joanne's deck, looking out over the Tweedsmuir River in Stainton, enjoying a cold drink. Joanne was a quiet woman who hesitated to say anything in public, but over the years Sarah had grown to respect her insight and spiritual depth. During a lull in the conversation, Joanne leaned forward and said, "We really aren't risking much anymore, are we? We seem to be playing it safe, don't we?"

Sarah was thrilled to hear Joanne say this; there was someone else who was seeing what Sarah saw. So Sarah responded eagerly, "I think you're right, I have been feeling the same way for a while." Then cautiously she went on: "Would you be willing to say what you have just said at the next elders' meeting?" Joanne blanched. Sarah, knowing that speaking in public was difficult for Joanne, said, "Because you don't often speak at the elders' meetings, I am sure people will listen carefully to what you have to say. Your voice needs to be heard, because you have recognized something that I am not sure any of the other elders are seeing." Finally, with some further gentle encouragement from Sarah, Joanne agreed to share her insights the next time the elders gathered.

Joanne had her opportunity to speak about what she had been seeing and thinking about two weeks after the conversation on the back deck. During the part of the meeting when elders could raise concerns, Joanne spoke up. She said, "When Sarah came, we were willing to try a number of things, things that we had never done before. We even took on some projects that pushed us out of our comfort zone. I am not sure we are willing to take risks anymore. We think we are safe—with money in the bank, a minister whom we like, and new people coming. But we have no passion. It was better before, when we were not sure that we were going to make it." The other elders were attentive as Joanne spoke; this was the most she had ever said at a meeting.

Bill, who was in his thirties and had been an elder for less than two years, was the first to jump into the silence that followed Joanne's words. "You're right," he said. "We have become too complacent. We need to do some new things. We need a good shake-up around here."

Wise as always, Alec joined the conversation, "If we are going to take on new initiatives, we will have to stop doing some of the things we are doing right now. Or we won't be able to do the new projects well. What are we going to stop doing?"

Joanne quietly asked, "So you are saying some things have to die so that we can find new life and energy?"

"Think about the Women's Missionary Society," Heather said. A woman in her early seventies, Heather was part of every women's group in the church. She thought of herself as part of the women's groups first, and as an elder second. "Last year we wrote you a letter saying we didn't have the energy to do our meetings the way we had been doing them. We asked if it was OK for us to stop using the educational resources sent from the national office. We just wanted to get together for fellowship and a cup of tea. You said that would be fine. The WMS died and was reborn as something different.

"My sister was telling me about the Sunday school at the church she goes to," Heather continued. "They had almost no kids coming, and everyone thought the Sunday school was about to die. Someone said they should stop having Sunday school and try an after-school program once a month on a weekday afternoon. So they closed the Sunday school, and now they have twenty or thirty children coming to their after-school program. The Sunday school died, and something else has been born."

There was a pause as people thought about what Heather had said. Finally, Sarah spoke. "Jesus did say that we needed to take up our cross and follow him. Taking up the cross means dying. Maybe there are things that have to die here at St. John's, so we can find new life."

Roger, who was in his mid-seventies, asked with a defensive tone in his voice, "What are you talking about? We have to maintain the traditions of this church. Isn't that part of our job?"

"Well," Joanne mused, "maybe it is more that we have to die to what we think St. John's is as a church. Like, is it possible to be elected an elder even if you didn't grow up in this church? Or can there be things in the worship service that do not need to fit what I think a worship service should be each Sunday? Letting go of those habits would be a kind of dying, wouldn't it?"

As Sarah sat listening to what was being said, she was thanking God for the privilege of working with such spiritually discerning leaders. Sarah also recognized that she was called to challenge the elders to move beyond talk. "What here at St. John's is dying? And are we stopping that death from happening? If new life comes out of death, then we should stop getting in the way of those deaths taking place. But maybe that is the wrong question to begin with. I have been wondering if there are things in me that need to die, so the new life God brings can be seen. And that got me thinking about whether there are things we as elders do, like what Joanne mentioned, that need to die so new life can come."

This was a breakthrough meeting for St. John's and for Sarah. Much more discussion and debate would follow in the weeks and months to come about what it meant for a church and for the leaders of a church to die. But the elders had reached a consensus that playing it safe, simply working to maintain the structures that existed, was not an option. While there might have been conversation about which cross St. John's was called to bear, there was a deep understanding that cross-bearing, being willing to die so that God might make the church alive again, was to be the congregation's way of life.

On a cold afternoon in early December, Sarah was again visiting Joanne. They were drinking hot chocolate at Joanne's kitchen table. Sarah said, "Thank you for having the courage to say what you did at the elders' meeting six months ago." Joanne smiled, "Thank you for pushing me to speak." She went on, "It is easy to forget that it is in dying that we are given new life. Maybe we should have a refresher about this every year. But you can do the talking next time." Sarah laughed. As Sarah headed for home she rejoiced in a God who can be trusted to get dead congregations out of the grave.

Notes

PROLOGUE

1. Charles M. Olsen, *Transforming Church Boards into Communities of Spiritual Leaders* (Herndon, VA: Alban Institute, 1995).

2. Sonja M. Stewart and Jerome W. Berryman, *Young Children and Worship* (Louisville: Westminster John Knox, 1989).

3. C. S. Lewis, *The Last Battle: A Story for Children* (Harmondsworth, Middlesex: Puffin Books, 1964; orig. pub. 1956), 155.

CHAPTER 1

1. Michael Jinkins, *The Church Faces Death: Ecclesiology in a Post-Modern Context* (New York: Oxford University Press, 1999), 12.

2. Ibid., 14.

3. Leonard Sweet, *Soul Tsunami: Sink or Swim in New Millennium Culture* (Grand Rapids: Zondervan, 1999).

4. G. K. Chesterton, "The Five Deaths of the Faith," in *The Everlasting Man* (original: New York: Dodd, Mead and Company, 1925; reprinted, Westport, CT: Greenwood Press, 1974), 312.

5. Kenneth Scott Latourette, *A History of the Expansion of Christianity, vol. 7: Advance Through Storm* (New York: Harper & Brothers, 1945), 418-419.

6.   I first heard Andrew Walls make these comments as part of a panel at the 1999 American Academy of Religion conference held in Toronto. Subsequently I have heard him make similar comments.

7.   Aubrey Malphurs, *Pouring New Wine into Old Wineskins: How to Change a Church without Destroying It* (Grand Rapids: Baker Books, 1993). This is an ironic choice of title. Jesus's point (Matt. 9:17) is that new wine cannot go into old wineskins—new wineskins alone can hold new wine. A made-new church will of necessity destroy the old skins of the previous church, if the made-new church is to reach the potential God envisions for it.

8.   Kennon L. Callahan, *Twelve Keys to an Effective Church: Strategic Planning for Mission* (San Francisco: Harper & Row, 1983), xiii.

9.   Ibid., xx.

10.   Ibid., xxi.

11.   Christian Schwarz, *Natural Church Development: How your congregation can develop the eight essential qualities of a healthy church* (orig. Emmelsbull, Germany: C&P Publishing, 1996; Canadian edition, Winfield, British Columbia: The Leadership Center, 2002).

12.   David Poling-Goldenne and L. Shannon Jung, *Discovering Hope: Building Vitality in Rural Congregations* (Minneapolis: Augsburg-Fortress, 2001).

13.   Robert Dale, *To Dream Again: How to Help Your Church Come Alive* (Nashville: Broadman Press, 1981).

14.   Alice Mann, *Can Our Church Live? Redeveloping Congregations in Decline* (Herndon, VA: Alban Institute, 1999).

15.   Ibid., 7.

16.   Brian McLaren, *The Church on the Other Side: Doing Ministry in the Postmodern Matrix* (Grand Rapids: Zondervan, 1998), 26.

17.   Mary K. Sellon, Daniel P. Smith, and Gail F. Grossman, *Redeveloping the Congregation: A How To for Lasting Change* (Herndon, VA: Alban Institute, 2002), xii.

18.   Stephen Compton, "From Birth to Death: Exploring the Life Cycle of the Church," *Congregations,* Fall 2003, 32-36. For a more detailed discussion of Compton's prescription for turnaround of mainline denominations in North America, see *Rekindling the Mainline: New Life through New Churches* (Herndon, VA: Alban Institute, 2003).

19.   Bill Easum, *Dancing with Dinosaurs: Ministry in a Hostile and Hurting World* (Nashville: Abingdon, 1993) and *Sacred Cows Make Gourmet Burgers: Ministry Anytime, Anywhere, by Anyone* (Nashville: Abingdon, 1995).

20.   And they have written a book together, *Growing Spiritual Redwoods* (Nashville: Abingdon, 1997). See also www.bandy.com.

21.   Easum, *Dancing with Dinosaurs,* 41.

22.   Thomas Bandy, *Kicking Habits: Welcome Relief for Addicted Churches* (Toronto: United Church Publishing House, 1997). Easum wrote the foreword to this book.

23.   Bill Easum, *Leadership on the OtherSide: No Rules, Just Clues* (Nashville: Abingdon, 2000); and Thomas Bandy, *Christian Chaos: Revolutionizing the Congregation* (Nashville: Abingdon, 1999).

24.   C. Hoekendijk, *The Church Inside Out,* L.A. Hoedemaker and Pieter Tijmes, eds.; Isaac C. Rottenberg, trans. (Philadephia: Westminster, 1964; trans. 1966), 71-83.

25.   Martin E. Marty, with Paul R. Biegner, Roy Blumhorst, and Kenneth R. Young, *Death and Birth of the Parish* (St. Louis: Concordia, 1964), 7.

26.   Ibid., vi.

27.   Ibid., 30.

CHAPTER 2

1.   This insight is more fully outlined in Dale Davis, *Judges: Such a Great Salvation* (Fearn, Scotland: Christian Focus Publications, 2000; previously published, Grand Rapids: Baker Book House, 1990 and 1991), 139-152, esp. 145-146.

2.   Jim Collins, *Good to Great: Why Some Companies Make the Leap . . . and Others Don't* (New York: HarperCollins, 2001), 83-87.

3.   Jinkins, *The Church Faces Death,* 28.

4.   Ibid.

5.   Ronald A. Heifetz and Marty Linsky, *Leadership on the Line: Staying Alive through the Dangers of Leading* (Boston: Harvard Business School Press, 2002), 11.

6.   Ibid., 30.

7. For further discussion of the need to "join" the church in order to lead the congregation, see R. Paul Stephens and Phil Collins, *The Equipping Pastor: A Systems Approach to Congregational Leadership* (Herndon, VA: Alban Institute, 1993).

CHAPTER 3

1. Heifetz and Linsky, *Leadership on the Line,* 31-48.
2. Marshall McLuhan and Quentin Fiore, *The Medium Is the Massage: An Inventory of Effects* (Toronto: Bantam Books, 1967), 93.
3. Swiss-born psychiatrist Elisabeth Kübler-Ross famously set forth what she called "the five stages of grief" in her classic *Death and Dying* (New York: Simon & Schuster/Touchstone, 1969).
4. Brian Moore, *No Other Life* (Toronto: Vintage Book Canada, 1994), 173-174.
5. Ben Campbell Johnson and Andrew Dreitcer, *Beyond the Ordinary: Spirituality for Church Leaders* (Grand Rapids: Eerdmans, 2001), 8-9.

CHAPTER 4

1. Alan E. Lewis, *Between Cross and Resurrection: A Theology of Holy Saturday* (Grand Rapids: Eerdmans, 2001), 23.
2. The authors in Beth Ann Gaede, ed., *Ending with Hope: A Resource for Closing Congregations* (Herndon, VA: Alban Institute, 2002) highlight the courage and grace exhibited by leaders and church members in congregations that are closing their doors. They are truly able to end in the hope of the resurrection.
3. Jeffrey M. Burns, "Que es esto? The Transformation of St. Peter's Parish, San Francisco, 1913-1990," in James P. Wind and James W. Lewis, eds., *American Congregations, vol. 1: Portraits of Twelve Religious Communities* (Chicago: University of Chicago Press, 1994), 396-463.
4. Burns, "Que es esto?," 422.
5. This story is put together from conversations and e-mail correspondence with David Sherbino, along with figures taken from *The Acts*

and Proceedings of the General Assembly of The Presbyterian Church in Canada, 1962 (488-489), 1993 (701), and 2006 (693).

6. Jinkins, *The Church Faces Death,* 102-103.

7. Ibid., 103.

8. St. Andrew's Church's story is from the author's notes.

9. Julia Esquivel, *Threatened with Resurrection: Prayers and Poems from an Exiled Guatemalan* (Elgin, IL: Brethren Press, 1982), 59-63.

10. Ibid.

11. Parker Palmer, *The Active Life: Wisdom for Work, Creativity, and Caring* (San Francisco: HarperSan Francisco, 1990), 143-150, cf. esp. 146. While I disagree with Palmer about who is threatening the writer and reader with resurrection, I do appreciate this fascinating comment: "All this ambiguity finally seems profoundly reassuring to me. It suggests that all forces in life, those of death as well as of life, may work ultimately for good, whether they intend to or not. Ultimately, both the gorillas and the martyrs act toward the same end, the end of new life through resurrection (although the gorillas, with their insensitivity to life, may never realize that grace)" (148).

12. Esquivel, *Threatened with Resurrection.*

13. Ibid.

14. Ibid.

15. The story is gleaned from the keynote address at the Renewal Fellowship within the Presbyterian Church in Canada Annual Meeting, March 3, 2007, held in Streetsville, Ontario.

CHAPTER 5

1. Norman Ellis, *My Parish Is Revolting* (Don Mills, Ontario: PaperJacks, 1974), see esp. 13-27.

2. "Bethel Munro church celebrates 100 years," *Mitchell Advocate,* May 28, 2003, 8.

3. This story is put together from articles in the *Mennonite Brethren Herald:* "Personalia," vol. 42, no. 14 (Oct. 24, 2003); and "New Church Starts," vol. 43, no. 2 (Feb. 6, 2004).

4. Author's notes.

CHAPTER 6

1. *The Rule of St. Benedict in English* (Collegeville, MN: Liturgical Press, 1982), chapter 4, 46-47.

2. This story is put together from the author's notes and conversations with congregation members.

3. *Cotton Patch Gospel: The Greatest Story Ever Told: A toe-tapping full-length musical* (Chicago: Dramatic Pub., 1982); book by Tom Key and Russell Treyz; music and lyrics by Harry Chapin; based on Clarence Jordan, *The Cotton Patch Version of Matthew and John* (New York: Association Press, 1970).

4. *End of the Spear,* film directed by Jim Hanon; produced by William Bowling and Bill Ewing; screenplay by Bill Ewing, Bart Gavigan, and Jim Hanon; distributed by Every Tribe entertainment. The film is based on Steve Sant, *End of the Spear: A True Story* (Carol Stream, IL: Tyndale House Publishers, 2005). See also Elisabeth Elliot, *Through Gates of Splendor: The Martyrdom of Five Missionaries in the Ecuador Jungle* (New York: Harper, 1957).

www.ingramcontent.com/pod-product-compliance
Lightning Source LLC
Chambersburg PA
CBHW020356270326
41926CB00007B/460